CO-ARCHITECTS OF GROWTH

BISWAJIT SALUI

Chennai • Bangalore

CLEVER FOX PUBLISHING
Chennai, India

Published by CLEVER FOX PUBLISHING 2026

ISBN: 978-93-7500-739-5

Author Information:

Biswajit Salui A polymath at heart, he brings many years of illustrious experience working with a multinational conglomerate, where he has mastered the art of navigating intricate corporate ecosystems and cultivating transformative solutions. His journey through diverse organizational landscapes has provided him with profound insights into the often-overlooked yet pivotal dynamics of Creator-Growth Catalyst Synergy relationships.

An ardent seeker of wisdom, Biswajit is deeply immersed in the realms of science, spirituality, and the written word—interests that have shaped his unique perspective on workplace synergy. Blending analytical rigor with soulful exploration, he seeks to unravel the hidden layers of collaboration, trust, and empowerment that define thriving professional partnerships. His fascination with the human spirit's boundless potential finds expression in his writing, where he draws parallels between universal truths and workplace harmony. Biswajit's upcoming exploration, "Co-Architects of Growth: Redefining Creator-Growth Catalyst Synergy", is a testament to his commitment to decoding and reimagining the symbiotic alliance between employees and managers.

With a vision to inspire organizations to craft empowered, trust-driven cultures, Biswajit aspires to leave an indelible mark on the evolving narrative of leadership and teamwork. Foreword

In the intricate web of professional relationships, none is as foundational or as transformative as the bond between employees and their managers. This unique dynamic—often fraught with challenges and brimming with potential—holds the power to shape not just individual careers but entire organizations. Yet, in many workplaces, this relationship remains underexplored, leading to missed opportunities for growth, trust, and innovation.

Co-Architects of Growth: Redefining Creator-Growth Catalyst Synergy is more than a book; it is a profound exploration into the symbiotic connection between these two pivotal roles. Drawing from over 18 years of experience within the complex ecosystems of a multinational conglomerate, Biswajit Salui brings to life a compelling narrative that combines practical wisdom with philosophical depth. His journey has allowed him to observe firsthand the transformative impact of empowered partnerships and the cost of disconnected leadership.

What sets this work apart is Biswajit's ability to merge diverse disciplines—corporate insights, scientific principles, and spiritual reflections—to offer a fresh perspective on leadership. The book delves into how trust, collaboration, and mutual growth can turn the Creator-Growth Catalyst Synergy relationship into a co-creative force. By addressing the unspoken challenges and offering actionable solutions, it provides a roadmap for professionals seeking to navigate the complexities of modern workplaces with grace and impact.

As you turn these pages, you'll uncover stories of resilience, principles rooted in timeless truths, and strategies that challenge conventional norms. Biswajit's narrative encourages leaders to rethink their role not as controllers but as co-architects of success, and employees to view themselves as proactive collaborators in shaping their career journeys.

This book arrives at a critical moment when workplaces are redefining themselves in the face of global shifts, and the need for authentic, harmonious relationships is greater than ever. Whether you are a seasoned leader, a budding professional, or someone intrigued by the interplay of human connection and organizational success, this book offers profound insights that will leave you both inspired and equipped to act.

Biswajit Salui's voice is a much-needed addition to the discourse on workplace relationships, and Co-Architects of Growth is destined to become a cornerstone for building cultures of trust, empowerment, and mutual success. It is not just a book, it is a movement, inviting us all to co-create workplaces where everyone thrives together. Let this journey begin.

PREFACE

The workplace is more than a collection of desks, projects, and processes—it is a living ecosystem, where individuals bring their hopes, challenges, and untapped potential. At the heart of this eco system lies a relationship so fundamental, yet so often neglected, that its impact resonates across every facet of organizational success: the bond between an employee and their manager. This relationship is not just transactional; it is transformative. When nurtured with intention, it becomes a powerful force, capable of shaping careers, sparking innovation, and redefining the culture of entire organizations. Yet, all too often, this dynamic remains fraught with misunderstanding, misaligned expectations, and missed opportunities.

Co-Architects of Growth: Redefining Creator-Growth Catalyst Synergy is a call to rethink this relationship. It is an exploration into the extraordinary potential that emerges when employees and managers step beyond traditional roles and embrace their shared power to co-create something far greater than the sum of its parts.

This book stems from my 18-year journey through the labyrinthine corridors of a multinational conglomerate. During this time, I observed a recurring theme: workplaces flourish when the employee-manager dynamic transcends hierarchy and becomes a true partnership. I saw relationships where trust became the foundation of excellence and others where the absence of synergy stifled growth. These observations ignited a desire to decode this relationship, to understand what makes it thrive, and to share those insights with a broader audience.

===

But this is no ordinary workplace guide. Co-Architects of Growth is a deeply reflective and multi-dimensional journey that draws from disciplines as diverse as science, spirituality, and human behavior. It challenges the reader to see beyond conventional boundaries and embrace a more innovative, holistic approach to professional relationships.

Here's what makes this book different:

1. An Evolutionary Perspective:
   It explores the evolution of workplace dynamics, shifting from rigid hierarchies to fluid, co-creative partnerships. This is not about managers "leading" employees but about both parties co-architecting success in an equitable and empowering way.
2. The Alchemy of Trust:
   Trust is not just a soft skill—it is the most powerful currency in professional relationships. Through nuanced insights and actionable strategies, the book examines how trust is built, maintained, and leveraged for exponential growth.
3. Energy as the New Metric:
   Drawing from both science and spirituality, the book introduces the concept of energetic leadership—the idea

that relationships thrive when individuals align their energies toward shared goals, creating harmony and momentum.

4. Conflict as a Catalyst:
   It reimagines conflict not as a roadblock but as an opportunity for reinvention. By confronting challenges head-on, employees and managers can emerge with deeper understanding and stronger bonds.
5. A Universe of Stories:
   Woven throughout are real, untold stories of Creator-Growth Catalyst Synergy dynamic stories of triumph, failure, and transformation. These narratives offer not only inspiration but also valuable lessons for readers to reflect upon and apply.
6. Practical Innovation:
   Each chapter introduces groundbreaking tools and frameworks to help readers redefine their approach to communication, feedback, and collaboration. From energy-mapping techniques to reflective exercises, the book equips you with resources that are as original as they are effective.
7. The Bigger Picture:
   This book goes beyond the microcosm of individual relationships to explore their ripple effect on organizational culture, societal progress, and even personal fulfillment.

The relationship between an employee and a manager is like a seed: it holds the potential to grow into a thriving tree, bearing fruits of innovation, trust, and mutual success. But for that seed to flourish, it requires care, alignment, and an unwavering belief in shared purpose. Co-Architects of Growth is not just about improving workplace relationships; it is about reimagining what they can become. It is about moving from ordinary to extraordinary, from transactional to transformative. It is an invitation to managers and employees alike to co-create a workplace where every interaction builds bridges, fosters growth, and ignites shared brilliance. As you turn these pages, I invite you to step into a new narrative—one where trust is the foundation, collaboration is the strategy, and growth is the inevitable outcome. Together, let us redefine what it means to thrive in the modern workplace.

Welcome to the symphony of synergy. Welcome to Co-Architects of Growth.

Name: Biswajit Salui

Education: Master of Business Administration & Empaneled Independent Director of IICA Data Bank

Email: Biswajit.salui@gmail.com/Mob:9830920920

Edition:I

Place-Kolkata, India

===

CONTENTS

PART 1

FOUNDATIONS OF SYNERGY

1

THE POWER OF CONNECTION

In the complex web of professional relationships, the connection between an employee and a manager serves as the cornerstone of organizational success. This bond transcends mere transactions; it becomes the lifeblood of trust, collaboration, and growth. Yet, how often is this connection overlooked, reduced to task assignments and performance reviews?

This chapter explores the psychology of human connection and its transformative impact on workplaces. It delves into:

Relational Resonance: The subtle, almost invisible alignment that occurs when trust and respect are nurtured.

Emotional Microcurrents: How small, consistent gestures—like active listening or a simple acknowledgment—can ripple through an entire team, creating waves of positivity. Connection Over Correction: Shifting from a problem-fixing mindset to one that focuses on strengthening bonds.

By the end of this chapter, we'll understand that true synergy begins not with policies or strategies but with the simple yet profound act of seeing each other as people first.

The Synergy Equation can be defined as:

Synergy (S) = (C × T × U) ÷ (R + E)

Where:

C = Connection (the strength of relationships between individuals)

T = Trust (the degree of confidence and psychological safety)

U = Understanding (the level of empathy, communication, and shared purpose) R = Roles (rigid adherence to hierarchical or transactional roles)

E = Ego (the influence of self-interest over collective goals)

This equation captures the dynamics required for synergy in the workplace, where strong connections, trust, and understanding are amplified when roles and ego are minimized.

Real-Life Examples Proving the Equation

Example 1: Google's Psychological Safety (High Synergy)

Scenario: Google's Project Aristotle revealed that psychological safety—trust within teams—was the key to high-performing groups. Employees felt safe to take risks, voice ideas, and admit mistakes without fear of judgment.

C (Connection): Strong interpersonal relationships among team members fostered open communication.

T (Trust): High trust ensured everyone felt valued and respected.

U (Understanding): Shared goals and empathy for one another's challenges created alignment. R (Roles): Low rigidity; team members often stepped beyond formal roles to contribute where needed.

E (Ego): Low; contributions were valued regardless of hierarchy or position. Outcome (S): High synergy enabled teams to collaborate effectively and innovate consistently, outperforming less connected teams.

Example 2: Pixar's Braintrust Model (High Synergy, Low Ego)

Scenario: Pixar's Braintrust meetings allow creators to share work-in-progress films with trusted colleagues for feedback. Criticism focuses on improving the project, not on individual shortcomings.

C (Connection): Strong relationships between creators foster open dialogue. T (Trust): High trust enables candid feedback without defensiveness.

U (Understanding): Empathy and shared commitment to the project ensure constructive criticism. R (Roles): Low rigidity; feedback comes from anyone in the room, not just leaders. E (Ego): Low; feedback focuses on the work, not individual pride.

Outcome (S): The Braintrust model creates a high-synergy environment where great films are born from collaborative refinement.

Example 3: NASA Apollo 13 (Crisis Synergy)

Scenario: After an explosion jeopardized the Apollo 13 mission, NASA engineers and astronauts collaborated under intense pressure to save lives and bring the crew home. C (Connection):

A strong sense of unity and teamwork drove collaboration. T (Trust): Astronauts trusted engineers, and engineers trusted each other's expertise. U (Understanding): Everyone aligned on the singular goal of bringing the crew home safely. R (Roles): Flexible; team members took on roles outside their formal responsibilities to solve problems.

E (Ego): Nonexistent; personal pride was set aside for the mission's success. Outcome (S): High synergy saved the lives of the Apollo 13 crew and became a legendary example of crisis collaboration

Example 4: Spotify Squad Model (Balanced Synergy)

Scenario: Spotify's Squad model empowers small, cross-functional teams to own specific features or projects, operating like independent start-ups within the organization.

C (Connection): Strong relationships within squads promote collaboration. T (Trust): Squads have autonomy, and leadership trusts their decisions.

U (Understanding): Shared purpose within squads aligns efforts and reduces friction. R (Roles): Flexible; members often contribute beyond their defined roles. E (Ego): Low; the focus is on the squad's goals, not individual recognition. Outcome (S): The model supports rapid innovation and adaptability, ensuring Spotify remains competitive in a fast-changing market.

Key Takeaways from the Equation:

High C, T, and U: Strong connections, trust, and understanding maximize synergy.

Low R and E: Minimizing rigid roles and ego removes barriers to collaboration. Balancing Inputs: The equation emphasizes the interplay of human relationships, mutual respect, and flexibility to create environments where synergy thrives.

This equation demonstrates that foundational elements like connection, trust, and understanding must outweigh the constraints of rigid roles and ego for organizations to achieve sustainable success.

🎬 Why Relationships Drive Workplace Success

Strong workplace relationships are the foundation of trust, collaboration, and innovation. They transform the workplace from a space of transactional exchanges into an ecosystem of growth and fulfillment. Relationships, when prioritized, create a ripple effect that impacts not just individual performance but also the overall organizational culture.

Key Insights:

Relationships Build Resilience: In times of uncertainty or crisis, strong relationships act as the glue that holds teams together. Employees who feel connected to their managers and peers are more likely to weather challenges with optimism and perseverance.

Human Connection Fuels Innovation: Creativity flourishes in environments where individuals feel safe to express themselves without fear of judgment. Strong relationships foster a sense of psychological safety, allowing employees to think boldly and innovate freely.

Engagement Starts with Connection: Gallup studies consistently show that employees who feel connected to their managers are significantly more engaged and productive. Relationships are the bridge between personal motivation and organizational objectives.

Relationships Reduce Turnover: Employees leave managers, not companies. When managers build genuine relationships with their teams, it reduces turnover by fostering a sense of belonging and purpose.

Actionable Insight: Relationships don't need grand gestures to thrive. Simple, consistent actions like meaningful check-ins, authentic appreciation, and active listening can create profound, lasting connections.

🎬 Simple Truths About Trust and Understanding

Trust and understanding are not abstract ideals; they are tangible forces that shape the dynamics of every workplace interaction. Without them, workplaces develop into silos of suspicion and dis engagement. With them, teams transform into empowered units capable of achieving extraordinary results.

Key Insights About Trust:

Trust Grows Through Vulnerability: Managers and employees who can admit their mistakes, share their challenges, and ask for help build deeper connections. Vulnerability signals authenticity, which is the foundation of trust.

Trust is Reciprocal: It's a two-way street. Managers who trust their employees by giving them autonomy and employees who trust their managers by being open about their challenges create a virtuous cycle of trust.

Consistency is Key: Trust isn't built in a day but can be eroded in a moment. Consistently aligning actions with words, delivering on promises, and maintaining transparency are essential for trust building.

Key Insights About Understanding:

Understanding Starts with Curiosity: Genuine curiosity about a person's motivations, challenges, and goals fosters deeper understanding. It helps managers tailor their approach to the unique needs of each employee.

Empathy is an Understanding Multiplier: Empathy allows managers to step into their employees' shoes, making them better equipped to support and guide their teams.

Understanding Unveils Hidden Potential: Many employees have untapped skills and aspirations that only come to light when managers take the time to understand them.

Actionable Insight: Schedule regular one-on-one conversations not just to discuss performance but to understand individual aspirations, challenges, and motivations. This investment in understanding fosters long-term loyalty and trust.

Moving from Roles to Relationships.

The shift from rigid roles to meaningful relationships is transformative, both for individuals and organizations. Roles are functional; they define what a person does. Relationships, however, are foundational; they define who a person is within the team. When workplaces prioritize relation

ships over roles, they unlock a deeper level of engagement, collaboration, and mutual respect. Key Insights:

Roles are Static; Relationships are Dynamic: Roles focus on tasks and responsibilities, which remain relatively fixed. Relationships evolve, adapting to changing goals, challenges, and contexts. This adaptability is crucial in today's fast-paced workplaces.

Relationships Humanize Work: Viewing colleagues through the lens of relationships rather than roles shifts the focus from output to potential. It emphasizes the person behind the position, fostering empathy and collaboration.

Relationships Build Bridges Across Hierarchies: Traditional hierarchies often create barriers to communication and collaboration. Relationships break down these barriers, enabling open dialogue and shared ownership of outcomes.

Personal Investment Drives Professional Success: When managers invest in relationships, they create an environment where employees feel seen, valued, and supported. This sense of belonging directly impacts their willingness to go above and beyond in their roles.

Practical Shifts to Move from Roles to Relationships:

Learn the Stories Behind the Roles: Take the time to learn about employees' backgrounds, experiences, and aspirations. This understanding fosters deeper connections and reveals opportunities for growth.

Collaborate, Don't Dictate: Invite employees to contribute to decision-making processes. Co-creating solutions enhances their sense of ownership and strengthens relationships. Recognize the Person, Not Just the Performer: Celebrate personal milestones, acknowledge individual strengths, and support employees beyond their professional contributions.

Build Shared Goals: Create alignment between personal and organizational goals. This transforms the manager-employee dynamic into a partnership working toward a common vision. Micro-Moments Matter: Small, everyday interactions—greetings in the morning, words of encouragement, or a quick acknowledgment of effort—can have outsized impacts on relationship-building.

Authenticity Over Authority: Employees connect more with leaders who are authentic and approachable rather than distant and authoritative. Authenticity builds trust, which amplifies influence.

The Ripple Effect of Relationships: A strong Creator-Growth Catalyst Synergy relationship sets the tone for the entire team, influencing how colleagues interact, collaborate, and support one another. Cultural Sensitivity in Relationships: In diverse workplaces, understanding cultural differences in communication, motivation, and conflict resolution enhances relational synergy.

Actionable Insight: Redefine your leadership style by integrating relational touchpoints into daily workflows. Simple practices like starting meetings with personal check-ins or ending by integrating these insights into everyday interactions, workplaces can transform rigid, role-driven environments into thriving, relationship-first ecosystems that inspire trust, collaboration, and shared success.

2. Simple Truths About Trust and Understanding

   Simple Truths About Understanding:

   Understanding Begins with Listening: Listening isn't just hearing words; it's about grasping the emotions, intentions, and unspoken needs behind those words. This requires patience, attention, and empathy.

   Every Perspective Matters: Understanding grows when we respect diverse viewpoints and experiences. Valuing what each person brings to the table creates a culture of inclusivity and respect. Assumptions are Trust Killers: Misunderstandings arise when assumptions replace communication. Asking clarifying questions and seeking confirmation of intentions helps build true understanding.

   Key Takeaway: Trust and understanding are not complicated; they thrive on consistency, authenticity, and active effort. When cultivated, they transform workplaces into environments where individuals feel valued, seen, and empowered to contribute their best.

3. Moving from "Roles" to "Relationships"

   One of the most significant shifts in modern workplace dynamics is the transition from rigid roles to meaningful relationships. Traditional hierarchies defined interactions by roles— managers dictated, employees executed. But this approach misses the human essence of work. Today, thriving organizations focus on building relationships where roles are simply functional, but relationships are foundational.

Why This Shift Matters:

Roles Define Tasks; Relationships Build Engagement: A manager who sees an employee only as a job title will struggle to inspire engagement. On the other hand, a manager who invests in understanding the person behind the role fosters deeper commitment and motivation.

Relationships Encourage Growth Beyond Titles: Strong relationships create opportunities for mentorship, skill-building, and personal development. Employees feel supported to grow, even beyond their current roles, leading to greater loyalty and long-term success.

===

Breaking Down Hierarchical Walls: Relationships bridge the gap between authority and action. When managers and employees see each other as collaborators, it creates a more inclusive and dynamic workplace culture.

How to Move from Roles to Relationships:

Invest Time in Knowing Your Team: Understanding individual strengths, interests, and motivations helps managers engage with employees on a deeper level. For employees, taking the time to understand a manager's vision and challenges builds mutual respect.

Celebrate the Human Side of Work: Recognizing personal milestones, checking in on emotional well-being, and sharing moments of humor create bonds that go beyond job descriptions. Collaborate, Don't Dictate: Managers should involve employees in decision-making and problem-solving processes. This partnership approach demonstrates respect for their expertise and fosters a sense of ownership.

Focus on Shared Goals: Building relationships doesn't mean blurring boundaries; it means aligning efforts toward shared objectives. A relationship-based approach ensures everyone feels like a valued contributor to the bigger picture.

Real-World Example: A manager who views an employee as a "marketing specialist" may limit interactions to task assignments. But a manager who builds a relationship might discover the employee's hidden passion for data analytics and create opportunities for them to contribute in new, impactful ways.

Final Thoughts

The foundational principles of workplace synergy—relationships, trust, and moving beyond roles—are not just theoretical concepts. They are the bedrock of high-performing teams and thriving organizations. By investing in relationships, prioritizing trust, and focusing on understanding the individual, workplaces can transform into environments where everyone feels valued, engaged, and inspired to succeed.

🎬 The Shift from Control to Collaboration

The workplace of today is undergoing a profound transformation. The traditional leadership model, rooted in authority, control, and top-down management, is rapidly losing relevance in an era where creativity, agility, and collaboration define success. Employees no longer thrive under the watchful eyes of micromanagement; instead, they seek autonomy, shared purpose, and mean relationships with their leaders. The shift from control to collaboration is not just a trend— it is a necessity for sustainable growth and innovation.

🎬 How Traditional Leadership Models Are Evolving

Historically, leadership was often synonymous with command and control. Managers dictated tasks, set rigid goals, and evaluated performance against pre-determined metrics. While this approach worked in highly structured, industrial settings, it stifles the adaptability and creativity required in today's dynamic environments.

Here's how traditional leadership is evolving:

1. From Command to Facilitation:
   Leaders are transitioning from being taskmasters to enablers. Instead of focusing solely on what needs to be done, they focus on creating an environment where employees can excel. This includes providing resources, removing obstacles, and fostering psychological safety.

2. From Authority to Authenticity:
   Employees are no longer impressed by titles or hierarchical power. They value leaders who are genuine, transparent, and approachable. Authenticity fosters trust, making collaboration more natural and effective.
3. From Monitoring to Mentoring:
   Leadership is shifting from surveillance to support. Managers are embracing the role of mentors, guiding employees toward growth rather than merely evaluating their performance.
4. From Rigid Structures to Fluid Roles:
   Teams now operate in cross-functional, project-based setups where leadership is situational rather than hierarchical. This fluidity allows employees to take responsibility and share leadership responsibilities as needed.

Key Insight: Modern leadership is not about controlling people but empowering them. It's about leveraging collective intelligence and fostering an environment where everyone feels like a valued contributor.

2

SHARED RESPONSIBILITY: A NEW WAY FORWARD

The idea of shared responsibility challenges the outdated notion that managers alone are accountable for success. In collaborative workplaces, responsibility is distributed across the team, empowering employees to take ownership of their roles while contributing to shared goals. 1. The Partnership Model:

Collaboration transforms the manager-employee dynamic into a partnership. Managers and employees work together to identify objectives, solve problems, and achieve outcomes. This shared approach enhances accountability and mutual respect.

2. Empowered Decision-Making:
   Employees are encouraged to make decisions within their areas of expertise, reducing dependency on managers for every choice. This autonomy fosters a sense of ownership and increases engagement.
3. Collective Accountability:
   When responsibilities are shared, so are the outcomes—both successes and failures. This collective accountability builds

trust and reinforces the idea that every team member plays a vital role.

4. Building a Culture of Co-Creation:
   Shared responsibility thrives in environments where everyone's input is valued. Managers must actively seek employee perspectives, involve them in decision-making, and align their contributions with the larger vision.

Key Insight: Shared responsibility creates a sense of unity. When employees feel that their voices matter and their contributions are essential, they become more invested in the organization's success.

🎬 The Small Changes That Build Big Trust

Trust is the foundation of any successful collaboration, and it's often the small, consistent actions that make the biggest impact. Leaders who focus on building trust lay the groundwork for meaningful, long-lasting collaboration.

1. Consistent Communication:
   Regular check-ins and transparent updates foster open lines of communication. Employees should always feel informed about changes, priorities, and expectations.
2. Delegation with Confidence:
   Trust is demonstrated by giving employees the autonomy to manage tasks without constant oversight. Empowering them to take ownership signals confidence in their abilities.
3. Recognizing Effort, Not Just Results:
   Celebrating milestones and acknowledging progress, even when the final outcome isn't perfect, reinforces trust and motivation.

4. Admitting Mistakes:
   Leaders who admit their mistakes and take accountability create a culture where employees feel safe doing the same. This openness strengthens trust and encourages risk-taking.
5. Listening to Learn, Not to Respond:
   Active listening shows that leaders value their employees' perspectives. Simple acts, like asking for input or following up on suggestions, can significantly build trust.
6. Aligning Actions with Words:
   Consistence between what leaders say and what they do reinforces credibility. Even small inconsistencies can erode trust over time.

Example in Practice:

A manager who regularly holds team meetings to discuss shared goals, delegates meaningful tasks, and acknowledges team contributions is more likely to cultivate trust and collaboration than one who simply assigns tasks and monitors completion.

Final Thought: The transition from control to collaboration is not about relinquishing leadership but redefining it. It's about recognizing that true leadership lies in building partnerships, fostering shared responsibility, and creating an environment where trust flourishes and collaboration thrives. This is the future of work—and the key to sustainable success.

The Collaboration Equation

To effectively shift from control to collaboration, an innovative equation can help managers and employees align their efforts, foster trust, and share responsibility. Here's a practical yet symbolic equation:

$$C = (T + A) \times (R \div E)$$

Where:

C = Collaboration (The outcome of successful partnership and shared responsibility) T = Trust (The foundation for all interactions, built through consistency and authenticity) A = Autonomy (The freedom employees need to take ownership of their roles and contribute meaningfully)

15 Redefining Creator-Growth Catalyst Synergy

Co-Architects of Growth

R = Responsibility (The shared commitment to achieving mutual goals and accountability for outcomes)

E = Ego (The degree to which personal agendas or hierarchies hinder progress; collaboration in proves as ego diminishes)

Breaking Down the Equation:

1. Trust and Autonomy as Multipliers:
   Trust (T) and Autonomy (A) multiply the potential for collaboration. High levels of both create a space where employees feel empowered to act, knowing their manager supports them.
2. Shared Responsibility as a Key Driver:

Responsibility (R) ensures that collaboration is purposeful. Shared goals and accountability align everyone's efforts toward a common vision.

3. The Ego Factor:
   Ego (E) acts as a divisor—reducing collaboration when it dominates interactions. When individuals prioritize their personal agendas over collective goals, collaboration weakens. Keeping ego in check amplifies the positive effects of trust, autonomy, and responsibility. Example in Practice:

Scenario: A manager gives their team autonomy to tackle a new project, setting clear shared goals and providing regular feedback (trust). Each team member takes ownership of their tasks (responsibility) and works collaboratively, avoiding personal conflicts or power struggles (low ego). Using the equation:

High Trust (T) + High Autonomy (A) creates a strong foundation.

Shared Responsibility (R) adds alignment and focus.

Low Ego (E) minimizes barriers, maximizing collaboration (C).

Result: The team achieves their goals efficiently, innovates along the way, and strengthens their working relationships.

This equation emphasizes that collaboration is not just an outcome—it's a dynamic process requiring intentional actions to balance trust, autonomy, responsibility, and ego. 2.The Alchemy of Trust

Trust is often referred to as the glue that holds relationships together, but in reality, it is far more dynamic and foundational. Trust is the lifeblood of any synergistic workplace. It enables open communication, fosters collaboration, and fuels productivity. Without trust, even the most skilled teams fail to reach their full potential. With trust, teams transform into cohesive units capable of extraordinary achievements.

The Equation for Trust in Synergy

$$T = (C + R + Tm) \times (Tr \div B)$$

Where:

T = Trust

C = Consistency (delivering on promises and maintaining reliability over time) R = Respect (valuing diverse perspectives and treating others with dignity) Tm = Transparency (openness in communication, decision-making, and intentions) Tr = Time (trust strengthens with repeated positive interactions over time) B = Breaches (the frequency and severity of trust violations, such as dishonesty or broken com)

Breaking Down the Equation

1. Consistency (C):
   Trust is built through reliable, predictable behavior. Consistency in actions, decisions, and communication reassures team members that they can depend on one another.
2. Respect (R):
   Treating colleagues as equals, regardless of rank or role, fosters trust. Respecting differences in opinions, skills, and experiences strengthens bonds.

3. Transparency (Tm):
   Open communication—sharing information honestly and proactively—removes ambiguity and builds credibility.
4. Time (Tr):
   Trust deepens with repeated positive interactions. Time allows individuals to observe and confirm each other's intentions and capabilities.
5. Breaches (B):
   Trust is fragile. Breaches like dishonesty, favoritism, or failure to deliver on promises erode trust quickly. Repairing such breaches requires deliberate effort and acknowledgment. Practical Examples

Example 1: Building Trust through Consistency and Respect

Scenario:

A small startup assigns a new project to an employee who has just joined. The manager sets clear expectations, provides necessary resources, and checks in regularly to ensure progress while allowing autonomy.

Trust Equation Application:

C (Consistency): The manager consistently follows up on promises, such as providing tools and feedback on time.

R (Respect): The manager listens to the employee's ideas and incorporates them, demonstrating respect for their expertise.

Tm (Transparency): The manager shares the broader vision of the project, so the employee understands its importance.

Tr (Time): Over a few weeks, repeated positive interactions strengthen the employee's trust. B (Breaches): No breaches occur, so trust grows steadily.

Outcome:

The employee delivers exceptional results, feels valued, and builds trust in the manager's leadership.

Example 2: Sustaining Trust through Transparency

Scenario:

In a multinational corporation, a team faces budget cuts that threaten a key project. The leader immediately communicates the situation, explains the rationale, and invites team members to propose solutions.

Trust Equation Application:

C (Consistency): The leader consistently updates the team on budget changes and decisions. R (Respect): The leader treats team members as equal stakeholders by involving them in problem solving.

Tm (Transparency): The leader is upfront about challenges, sharing all relevant details openly.

Tr (Time): Over the duration of the project, transparency reinforces the team's trust in the leader. B (Breaches): No withholding of information or favoritism occurs, avoiding breaches. Outcome:

The team finds innovative ways to achieve project goals within the budget and builds stronger trust with the leader.

Example 3: Repairing Trust after a Breach

Scenario:

A senior manager unintentionally overlooks the contributions of a key team member during a presentation. The team member feels undervalued and distant as a result.

Trust Equation Application:

C (Consistency): The manager acknowledges the mistake publicly and commits to recognizing contributions consistently in the future.

R (Respect): The manager meets privately with the team member to express regret and appreciation for their efforts.

Tm (Transparency): The manager explains the oversight without excuses, emphasizing their intent to avoid such mistakes moving forward.

Tr (Time): Over time, the manager demonstrates changed behavior, reinforcing the apology with consistent actions.

B (Breaches): The initial breach is addressed directly and repaired through actions, reducing its long-term impact.

Outcome:

The team member forgives the oversight, feels valued again, and the relationship between the manager and the team strengthens.

The Neuroscience Behind Trust and Productivity

Trust is not just an emotional concept—it has measurable physiological and neurological impacts that influence workplace productivity:

1. Oxytocin Release:
   Trust triggers the release of oxytocin, the "bonding hormone," which promotes feelings of connection and reduces stress. When employees trust their managers, they are more likely to collaborate and share ideas.
2. Reduced Amygdala Activation:
   Low trust activates the brain's fear center (amygdala), leading to stress and defensive behavior. High trust reduces this response, fostering openness and creativity.
3. Prefrontal Cortex Engagement:
   In environments of trust, the brain's prefrontal cortex (responsible for decision-making and problem-solving) is more active. This leads to better focus, innovation, and critical thinking. 4. Dopamine and Motivation:
   Acts of trust, such as recognizing contributions or delegating responsibilities, release dopamine— a neurotransmitter linked to motivation and satisfaction.

Final Insights

Trust is not a static quality; it is a dynamic force that must be nurtured, protected, and repaired. By applying the trust equation $T = (C + R + Tm) \times (Tr \div B)$ and understanding the neuroscience behind it, leaders and teams can create environments where trust becomes the foundation of synergy, unlocking their full potential for collaboration and productivity.

🎬 Building a Foundation of Trust

Trust is the cornerstone of successful collaboration, as it fosters open communication, psychological safety, and mutual respect. Without trust, relationships become transactional and guarded, while with trust, they evolve into synergistic partnerships that drive collective success. Building a foundation of trust requires honesty, consistency, and intentional actions to create an environment where people feel safe to contribute, innovate, and grow.

Equation for Building Trust

$T = (H + C) \times (PS \div F)$

Where:

T = Trust (the foundation of collaboration)

H = Honesty (transparent and authentic communication)

C = Consistency (reliable actions and behaviors over time)

PS = Psychological Safety (a sense of security to express ideas and take risks without fear of judgment)

F = Fear (the degree to which fear of failure, judgment, or consequences exists; trust decreases as fear increases)

Breaking Down the Equation

1. Honesty (H):

   Transparency and authenticity in communication build credibility. Honesty about challenges, in intentions, and feedback fosters a culture where individuals feel respected and valued.

2. Consistency (C):
   Trust is earned through repeated, reliable actions. A leader's ability to follow through on promises and maintain integrity reinforces the trustworthiness of their words and behaviors.
3. Psychological Safety (PS):
   Creating an environment where individuals feel safe to speak up, share ideas, and admit mistakes without fear of criticism or retaliation is crucial for trust to thrive.
4. Fear (F):
   Fear is the enemy of trust. Reducing fear by addressing concerns, providing support, and fostering inclusivity helps to create a trusting and collaborative atmosphere.

Practical Examples

Example 1: Honesty and Transparency as Trust Builders

Scenario:

A project manager discovers that a key deadline may be missed due to unforeseen challenges. Instead of hiding the issue, they openly communicate the problem to their team, outlining the situation and seeking input on solutions.

Equation Application:

H (Honesty): The manager's transparent communication builds credibility and reinforces trust. C (Consistency): The manager has a track record of addressing challenges openly, which strengthens the team's confidence in their leadership.

PS (Psychological Safety): The manager encourages team members to contribute ideas without fear of blame, fostering a collaborative environment.

F (Fear): The manager minimizes fear by focusing on solutions rather than assigning blame.

Outcome (T):

The team rallies together, finds a viable solution, and develops stronger trust in their manager's leadership style.

Example 2: Consistency in Leadership

Scenario:

A leader consistently recognizes their team's efforts during meetings, provides timely feedback, and delivers on their promises.

Equation Application:

H (Honesty): The leader's praise and feedback are sincere and aligned with team performance. C (Consistency): The leader's actions are dependable, creating a stable and predictable environment.

PS (Psychological Safety): Team members feel safe to share their successes and challenges, knowing they will be met with constructive feedback.

F (Fear): Fear is minimized as the team trusts the leader to handle situations fairly and respectfully. Outcome (T):

The team becomes more engaged and proactive, knowing their leader values their contributions and will support their growth.

Example 3: Reducing Fear to Build Psychological Safety

Scenario:

An employee in a tech firm admits to making a mistake that could impact a project's timeline. Instead of reprimanding them, the manager appreciates their honesty and works with them to find a solution while using the incident as a learning opportunity for the team. Equation Application:

H (Honesty): The manager's appreciation for the employee's honesty reinforces mutual respect. C (Consistency): The manager consistently responds to mistakes with fairness and problem-solving, building long-term trust.

PS (Psychological Safety): The employee feels safe to report issues without fear of retaliation, encouraging transparency.

F (Fear): Fear is mitigated as the focus shifts from blame to improvement. Outcome (T):

The employee becomes more confident and proactive in their work, knowing their manager fosters a supportive environment.

🎬 Practical Steps to Create Psychological Safety

1. Normalize Mistakes as Learning Opportunities:
   Encourage team members to share challenges and lessons learned from mistakes without fear of blame.
   Example: A sales manager shares their own missed targets and the strategies they used to recover, creating an open culture.
2. Value Contributions Equally:
   Actively seek input from all team members and acknowledge their ideas. Example: During brainstorming sessions, leaders rotate facilitation to ensure every voice is heard.
3. Encourage Open Feedback Loops:
   Create regular opportunities for employees to give feedback, not just receive it.
   Example: A manager holds monthly feedback sessions to discuss what's working and what can improve in team dynamics.
4. Model Vulnerability:
   Leaders should share their own challenges, uncertainties, or mistakes to humanize themselves and build relatability.
   Example: A CEO openly discusses the company's financial challenges during a town hall, reinforcing transparency.
5. Celebrate Risk-Taking:
   Reward individuals or teams for taking calculated risks, even if they don't always succeed. Example: A marketing team is recognized for launching a bold campaign, regardless of its mixed results.

Key Takeaways

Honesty and consistency are the cornerstones of trust. Transparent communication and dependable actions reinforce confidence and respect.

Psychological safety transforms teams into spaces where people feel valued and empowered to contribute.

Reducing fear allows individuals to focus on collaboration and innovation, rather than self-presser

By applying the equation $T = (H + C) \times (PS \div F)$ and using practical steps, leaders and teams can build a strong foundation of trust that serves as the bedrock for long-term collaboration and success.

PART 2

THE DYNAMICS OF CONNECTION

3

THE ART OF EMPATHY IN LEADERSHIP

The dynamics of connection form the lifeblood of any successful team or organization. Beyond technical expertise, meaningful connections between employees and leaders foster trust, collaboration, and synergy. This section delves into the key elements that shape strong workplace connections and how they fuel organizational success.

Equation for The Dynamics of Connection

$C = (E + A + R) \times (T \div B)$

Where:

C = Connection (the strength of interpersonal relationships)

E = Empathy (the ability to understand and share the feelings of others)

A = Active Listening (focused and intentional

listening to understand, not just to respond

) R = Respect (valuing others' perspectives, skills, and contributions)

T = Trust (the foundation for all relationships, built over time)

B = Bias (prejudices or preconceived notions that hinder connection; connection improves as bias decreases)

Key Components of the Equation

Empathy is the cornerstone of human connection. It involves recognizing and understanding others' emotions, which creates a sense of validation and belonging.

2. Active Listening (A):
   Listening with the intent to truly understand, rather than just waiting to respond, fosters deeper communication and connection.
3. Respect (R):
   Respect for individuality and diversity in thought creates an inclusive environment where people feel valued.
4. Trust (T):
   Trust is the multiplier that enhances all other components. Without trust, empathy, listening, and respect have limited impact.
5. Bias (B):
   Bias, whether conscious or unconscious, acts as a barrier to authentic connections. Addressing and reducing biases unlocks the full potential of connection.

Practical Examples of The Dynamics of Connection

Example 1: Empathy in Leadership

Scenario:

A leader notices an employee struggling with both workload and personal challenges. Instead of focusing solely on deadlines, the leader engages the employee in a private conversation to understand their situation and provide support.

Equation Application:

E (Empathy): The leader acknowledges the employee's challenges and shows genuine concern. A (Active Listening): The leader listens without interrupting, allowing the employee to share their perspective.

R (Respect): The leader values the employee's honesty and prioritizes their well-being over immediate deliverables.

T (Trust): The employee feels safe to discuss personal challenges, which strengthens their trust in the leader.

B (Bias): The leader avoids judgment and preconceived notions about the employee's struggles. Outcome (C):

The employee feels supported, regains motivation, and delivers quality work once the immediate challenges are resolved. The connection between the leader and employee deepens, improving team morale.

Example 2: Active Listening in Team Collaboration

Scenario:

During a brainstorming session, a junior team member suggests an idea that initially seems unconventional. The team leader actively listens, encourages the idea, and asks clarifying questions to explore its potential.

Equation Application:

E (Empathy): The leader recognizes the courage it takes for a junior member to voice their ideas. A (Active Listening): By focusing on the idea without judgment, the leader ensures the team member feels heard.

R (Respect): The leader respects the team member's contribution and validates its importance.

T (Trust): The team member feels confident that their input is valued, which strengthens trust. B (Bias): The leader avoids dismissing the idea based on the team member's role or experience.

Outcome (C):

The team builds on the junior member's idea, leading to an innovative solution. This reinforces a culture of collaboration and inclusion.

Example 3: Respecting Diverse Perspectives

In a cross-cultural team meeting, a manager actively incorporates the perspectives of team members from different cultural backgrounds to create a global strategy.

Equation Application:

E (Empathy): The manager acknowledges the unique challenges and strengths each culture brings. A (Active Listening): The manager attentively listens to each team member's input without interrupting.

R (Respect): The manager emphasizes the value of diverse viewpoints in shaping a well-rounded strategy.

T (Trust): Team members trust the manager's commitment to inclusivity and fairness. B (Bias): The manager actively counters biases by ensuring equal consideration for all perspectives.

Outcome (C):

The resulting strategy is both innovative and inclusive, leveraging the full potential of the team's diversity. Team members feel respected and motivated to contribute in future projects. Example 4: Overcoming Bias to Build Connection

Scenario:

A manager realizes they have unintentionally overlooked a quieter employee's contributions during team meetings. The manager makes a conscious effort to involve the employee and provide opportunities for them to share their ideas.

Equation Application:

E (Empathy): The manager understands that introverted employees may need encouragement to speak up.

A (Active Listening): The manager attentively listens when the employee shares their ideas. R (Respect): The manager shows respect by valuing the employee's insights and implementing their suggestions.

T (Trust): The employee gains confidence in the manager's fairness and inclusivity. B (Bias): The manager actively reduces their bias toward more vocal team members. Outcome (C):

The employee becomes more engaged and proactive in team discussions, enhancing overall team collaboration and connection.

Key Takeaways

1. Empathy, active listening, and respect are the building blocks of meaningful connections. 2. Trust amplifies connection, while bias acts as a barrier that must be minimized. 3. Practical actions like listening attentively, validating diverse perspectives, and showing empathy create an environment where connections thrive.

By applying the equation $C = (E + A + R) \times (T \div B)$, leaders and teams can intentionally foster strong workplace connections that drive collaboration, innovation, and collective success.

5. Feedback That Inspires, Not Intimidates

Feedback is one of the most powerful tools for personal and professional growth when delivered effectively. Transforming feedback into a tool for empowerment requires a shift from criticism to constructive dialogue, fostering trust, openness, and collaboration. This section explores how to provide and receive feedback that inspires improvement, drives engagement, and creates a growth oriented culture.

Equation for Growth-Oriented Feedback

$G = (T + R + E) \times (C \div F)$

Where:

G = Growth (the impact of feedback on individual and team development) T = Timeliness (providing feedback at the right time when it can make the most impact) R = Relevance (feedback tied to specific behaviors, actions, or goals)

E = Empathy (delivering feedback with understanding and care)

C = Constructiveness (clear, actionable suggestions for improvement)

F = Fear (reducing fear of judgment, which hinders open communication and learning)

Breaking Down the Equation

1. Timeliness (T):
   Feedback is most effective when provided close to the observed behavior or event. Timely feedback ensures relevance and maximizes its impact.
2. Relevance (R):
   Feedback should address specific actions or outcomes rather than general traits or characteristics, making it actionable and meaningful.
3. Empathy (E):
   Understanding the recipient's perspective and delivering feedback with care ensures that it is received positively and fosters trust.

4. Constructiveness (C):
   Feedback should focus on solutions and improvements rather than merely pointing out flaws. Clear, actionable steps encourage growth.
5. Fear (F):
   Fear of judgment or retaliation diminishes the effectiveness of feedback. Creating a safe environment for open dialogue reduces this fear and encourages honest exchanges.

Practical Examples of Growth-Oriented Feedback

Example 1: Transforming Feedback into Empowerment

Scenario:

A team member delivers a presentation that contains valuable insights but lacks clarity in the visuals. The manager addresses this after the meeting.

Equation Application:

T (Timeliness): The manager provides feedback immediately after the presentation, while it's still fresh.

R (Relevance): The feedback focuses specifically on the clarity of visuals, not the overall presentation style.

E (Empathy): The manager acknowledges the effort and highlights the presentation's strong points before addressing areas for improvement.

C (Constructiveness): The manager suggests actionable steps, such as using simpler graphics and reviewing design best practices.

F (Fear): The manager emphasizes that feedback is meant to enhance future presentations, reducing fear of judgment.

Outcome (G):

The team member feels motivated to improve, implements the suggestions, and delivers a clearer, more impactful presentation next time.

Example 2: The Art of Constructive Criticism

Scenario:

A software developer submits a piece of code that meets functional requirements but lacks efficiency.

Equation Application:

T (Timeliness): The feedback is given during the next team review session to maintain relevance. R (Relevance): The critique focuses on the code's inefficiency, not the developer's overall skillset.

E (Empathy): The reviewer recognizes the developer's effort and explains that learning to optimize code is a growth opportunity.

C (Constructiveness): Specific examples of how to refactor the code for efficiency are provided, along with resources for improvement.

F (Fear): The developer is reassured that mistakes are part of the learning process, encouraging openness to feedback.

Outcome (G):

The developer improves their coding skills, becomes more confident, and contributes higher-quality work in future projects.

Example 3: Creating a Culture of Open Dialogue

Scenario:

In a team setting, a leader implements regular feedback sessions where both managers and employees exchange feedback in a structured, nonjudgmental environment.

Equation Application:

T (Timeliness): Feedback sessions are scheduled monthly, ensuring regularity. R (Relevance): Feedback is focused on recent projects or interactions to maintain specificity. E (Empathy): Both parties actively listen to each other's perspectives during the sessions.

C (Constructiveness): Feedback is framed as collaborative problem-solving, with actionable next steps for both sides.

F (Fear): Fear is reduced through ground rules that emphasize respect and confidentiality.

Outcome (G):

The team develops stronger communication skills, resolves issues proactively, and fosters a culture of mutual respect and continuous improvement.

Practical Steps to Create Growth-Oriented Feedback

1. Start with Positives:
   Begin with what was done well to build confidence and set a positive tone for the conversation.

Example: "Your presentation had a lot of valuable insights, and I especially liked how you outlined the key takeaways."

2. Be Specific and Direct:
   Focus on specific actions or outcomes rather than general traits or assumptions.
   Example: "The visuals could have been clearer. Adding simpler graphics might help the audience focus on your main points."
3. Provide Actionable Suggestions:
   Offer clear steps for improvement to empower the recipient.
   Example: "Next time, you could try using charts with fewer data points or adding labels to clarify the visuals."
4. Encourage Two-Way Dialogue:
   Invite the recipient to share their perspective and suggestions.
   Example: "How do you feel about this? Do you have any thoughts on how we could make this process smoother?"
5. Foster a Safe Environment:
   Reinforce that feedback is about improvement, not criticism.
   Example: "We all have areas to grow in, and this is just one way we can refine our approach together."

Key Takeaways

1. Feedback should empower, not demoralize. Empathy and actionable suggestions turn criticism into an opportunity for growth.
2. Consistency and timeliness ensure feedback is relevant and impactful.
3. A culture of open dialogue reduces fear and fosters mutual respect, making feedback an ongoing process rather than a one-time event.

By applying the equation $G = (T + R + E) \times (C \div F)$, leaders and teams can transform feedback into a powerful tool for personal and professional development, building stronger connections and driving continuous improvement.

6. Conflict as a Tool for Growth
   Conflict is often seen as a disruption, but when managed effectively, it becomes a powerful catalyst for growth, innovation, and stronger relationships. By reframing conflict as an opportunity for learning and collaboration, organizations can address underlying issues, drive innovation, and strengthen team dynamics. This final version explores practical strategies to embrace disagree

constructively, turn tension into teamwork, and understand the role of emotions in conflict resolution.

Conflict as a Mirror of Organizational Health

Conflicts are not merely disputes; they are indicators of deeper systemic issues, such as communication gaps, misaligned goals, or cultural differences. Leaders can leverage these conflicts to identify and address areas needing improvement

Key Insights:

1. Revealing Root Causes:
   Conflict often highlights inefficiencies or misalignments that need attention.
   Example: A disagreement between marketing and sales teams over lead prioritization exposes the need for better-defined criteria and shared goals.

2. Unveiling Cultural Disconnects:
   Disputes between departments or teams often reflect cultural or value-based misalignments.

Example: A clash between a hierarchical team and a flat-structured startup during a merger reveals the need to align on decision-making processes and shared values.

Simple Ways to Embrace Disagreements Constructively

Rather than avoiding or suppressing conflict, leaders can adopt constructive approaches to turn disagreements into opportunities for collaboration.

Strategies:

1. Separate the Issue from the Individual:
   Focus on solving the problem rather than assigning blame.
   Example: During a budget meeting, a manager mediates a conflict by directing the discussion toward solutions rather than personal disagreements.
2. Encourage Open Dialogue:
   Create safe spaces where employees feel comfortable expressing differing viewpoints.

   Example: Weekly team retrospectives provide a structured environment for airing grievances and discussing improvements
3. Frame Conflict as an Opportunity for Growth:

Shift the narrative from conflict being a "problem" to it being a "pathway to better solutions."
Example: A design team views differing opinions on a product feature as an opportunity to create a hybrid solution that satisfies multiple user needs.

Turning Tension Into Teamwork

Tension can often feel divisive, but with the right strategies, it can strengthen collaboration and foster unity.

Strategies:

1. Identify Shared Goals:
   Help conflicting parties see how their objectives align.
   Example: Engineers and product managers disagree on a project timeline. The leader reframes the conversation around their shared goal of delivering a high-quality product on schedule.
2. Use Collaborative Problem-Solving:
   Engage teams in joint brainstorming sessions to find creative solutions.
   Example: During a conflict over resource allocation, a team uses design-thinking workshops to identify overlapping needs and optimize resources.
3. Celebrate Resolutions:
   Recognize the team's effort in resolving conflicts and achieving results.
   Example: After resolving a conflict over campaign messaging, the marketing team celebrates the successful launch and learns from the process.

The Importance of Understanding Emotions in Conflict

Emotions often fuel workplace conflicts, and understanding these emotions is critical to managing disputes effectively.

1. Recognize and Address Emotional Triggers:
   Emotions are data points that signal deeper concerns.
   Example: A manager notices that an employee becomes defensive during team meetings. Through one-on-one discussions, they uncover the employee's fear of being undervalued.
2. Practice Emotional Agility:
   Teach teams to regulate emotions and respond constructively during conflict.
   Example: A heated discussion is de-escalated when a team leader remains calm, acknowledges the tension, and redirects the conversation to actionable solutions.
3. Validate Emotional Experiences:
   Acknowledge the emotions of all parties to build trust and understanding.
   Example: During a conflict about workload distribution, the leader says, "I understand that this feels overwhelming. Let's work together to create a fair solution."

Critical Example: Merging Cultures Post-Acquisition

Scenario:

A large corporation acquires a smaller, innovative startup. The larger company values structure and hierarchy, while the startup thrives on flexibility and flat decision-making. Employees clash over work styles, creating resentment and reduced productivity.

Steps to Convert Conflict Into Growth:

1. Recognize the Root Issue:
   Leadership acknowledges that the conflict stems from differing cultural values rather than individual behavior.
   Action: Host open forums to gather employee feedback and understand challenges.
2. Reframe the Conflict:
   Highlight how the differences can create a unique blend of innovation and scalability. Action: Showcase examples of successful integrations where structure and flexibility coexist.

3. Facilitate Open Dialogue:
   Create structured opportunities for employees from both cultures to share perspectives and propose solutions.
   Action: Conduct workshops to align on shared goals and operational processes.
4. Integrate Best Practices:
   Combine the strengths of both cultures to create a new, hybrid system.
   Action: Form cross-functional task forces to develop new workflows that incorporate agility and structure.
5. Celebrate Early Wins:
   Highlight successful collaborative efforts to build trust and moral
   Action: Publicly recognize a joint team that developed a new product blending the startup's creativity and the corporation's market reach.

Outcome:

The integration strengthens both companies, leading to increased innovation, efficiency, and employee engagement.

Key Takeaways

1. Conflict Reveals Opportunities for Growth:
   Disputes highlight inefficiencies, biases, and gaps that need addressing, creating pathways for improvement.
2. Collaboration Transforms Tension Into Progress:
   By aligning on shared goals and encouraging joint problem-solving, teams can turn disagreements into actionable solutions.
3. Emotions Must Be Managed With Care:
   Addressing emotions constructively fosters understanding, trust, and long-term relationship-building.
4. Leaders Shape the Outcome of Conflict:
   Effective leaders reframe conflict as an opportunity, model emotional intelligence, and create environments where growth emerges from challenges.

Final Thought: Conflict as a Catalyst

Conflict, when approached strategically, transforms from a source of frustration to a tool for innovation and connection. It offers organizations a chance to learn, adapt, and grow stronger, fostering a culture where differing opinions are not only welcomed but celebrated. With the right mindset,

conflict becomes the foundation for continuous improvement and success.

PART 3

UNLOCKING SHARED POTENTIAL

Shared potential is unlocked when individuals and teams align their skills, motivation, and goals with the organization's purpose. By creating meaning and connecting personal aspirations with the broader mission, organizations can cultivate engagement, innovation, and a sense of belonging. This section explores how purpose, impact, and alignment drive motivation and engagement.

1. Motivation Through Meaning
   Unique Perspective:
   True motivation stems from a sense of purpose rather than external rewards. When employees see how their work contributes to a meaningful goal, they feel empowered and committed. Organizations that invest in creating meaning foster an engaged and high-performing workforce.

A. The Power of Purpose in Driving Engagement

Key Insight:

Purpose transforms routine tasks into fulfilling experiences. Employees are more engaged when they understand why their work matters and how it impacts the organization and society.

Practical Strategies:

1. Communicate the "Why":
   Leaders should consistently connect tasks to the larger mission of the organization.
   Example: A healthcare company ensures that every employee—from administrative staff to doc tors—knows their work contributes to saving lives. A receptionist understands that

their friendly interactions make patients feel comfortable and cared for.

2. Celebrate Meaningful Wins:
   Highlight stories that showcase how the organization's efforts create value.
   Example: A non-profit organization shares success stories from communities they've helped, making employees proud of their contributions to societal change.
3. Incorporate Purpose Into Onboarding:
   Start by embedding purpose into employee orientation, helping new hires see how their role fits into the larger mission.
   Example: A renewable energy company introduces new employees to the environmental impact of their projects, emphasizing their shared role in combating climate change.

Outcome:

Purpose-driven organizations see higher levels of employee engagement, reduced turnover, and greater resilience during challenges.

B. Helping Employees See Their Impact on the Bigger Picture

Key Insight:

When employees see the tangible results of their work, they feel valued and motivated to contribute more. Bridging the gap between individual roles and organizational outcomes fosters a sense of belonging and pride.

Practical Strategies:

1. Visualize Impact:

Use metrics, stories, or visuals to demonstrate how employees' efforts contribute to outcomes.

Example: A logistics company creates dashboards showing how individual contributions (like timely deliveries) enhance customer satisfaction and operational efficiency.

2. Provide Direct Feedback:

   Share specific examples of how an employee's work has made a difference.

   33 Redefining Creator-Growth Catalyst Synergy

   Co-Architects of Growth

   Example: A software developer receives feedback that their new feature improved the user experience, resulting in a 20% increase in customer retention.

3. Invite Employees to Witness Outcomes:

   Create opportunities for employees to see the results of their work firsthand.

   Example: A furniture company invites employees to visit customers' homes to see how their products enhance comfort and functionality, fostering pride and connection.

Outcome:

Employees who see their impact develop a stronger emotional connection to their work, leading to greater satisfaction and productivity.

C. Aligning Personal Goals With Organizational Objectives

Key Insight:

Aligning individual aspirations with organizational goals creates a win-win situation. Employees feel their growth is valued, while organizations benefit from their enhanced commitment and performance.

Practical Strategies:

1. Conduct Goal-Setting Conversations:
   Regularly discuss employees' personal goals and find ways to align them with the organization's objectives.
   Example: A marketing professional's goal to learn analytics is supported by assigning them to a data-driven campaign, aligning with the company's focus on improving ROI.
2. Offer Career Development Opportunities:
   Provide training and mentorship programs that help employees grow in ways that also benefit the organization.
   Example: A finance company offers certifications in emerging fields like fintech, aligning employee development with organizational innovation goals.
3. Create Pathways for Advancement:
   Show employees how their current role can evolve into higher-impact positions.
   Example: A customer service representative is shown a career path to leadership by achieving milestones like mentoring new hires or leading small projects.
4. Empower Employees to Drive Organizational Goals:
   Give employees autonomy to propose and lead initiatives that align with both their passions and the company's mission.

Example: An environmentally conscious employee suggests implementing a recycling program at the office, supporting both their values and the company's sustainability efforts.

Outcome:

When employees see a clear path to achieving their goals while contributing to organizational success, they become more engaged, motivated, and loyal.

Integrated Practical Example: Motivation Through Meaning

Scenario:

A mid-sized software company is struggling with declining engagement among its support team. Employees feel their roles are repetitive and disconnected from the company's success.

Steps Taken:

1. Communicating Purpose:
   Leadership emphasizes how customer support enhances the user experience and ensures long-term customer retention, critical for the company's growth.
2. Visualizing Impact:
   35 Redefining Creator-Growth Catalyst Synergy

   Co-Architects of Growth
   Weekly team meetings highlight metrics showing how timely responses and problem resolutions have directly contributed to increased customer satisfaction scores and renewals.

3. Aligning Personal Goals:
   The company introduces a program where support team members interested in product development can participate in feedback loops, providing insights to engineers based on customer interactions.

Outcome:

Engagement increases as employees feel valued and see how their efforts directly influence the company's success. Several support team members transition into product development roles, reducing turnover and enhancing cross-departmental collaboration.

Key Takeaways

1. Purpose Drives Engagement:
   Employees are more motivated and committed when they understand the "why" behind their work.
2. Impact Builds Connection:
   Showing employees how their efforts contribute to the organization's goals fosters pride and longing.
3. Alignment Fuels Growth:
   Aligning personal aspirations with organizational objectives creates a mutually beneficial dynamic that drives engagement and performance.

By unlocking shared potential through motivation, organizations create a thriving workplace where individuals feel connected, valued, and inspired to excel. This synergy not only enhances individual satisfaction but also drives collective success.

6

AUTONOMY AND ACCOUNTABILITY: THE PERFECT BALANCE

Balancing autonomy and accountability is critical for fostering innovation, engagement, and productivity in the workplace. When employees are given the freedom to explore and make decisions within a framework of accountability, it creates a culture of ownership and responsibility. This section elaborates on how to strike this balance, with unique benefits and practical examples.

1. Giving Freedom While Maintaining Focus

Key Insight:

Autonomy enables creativity and innovation, while accountability ensures alignment with organizational goals. By setting clear expectations and boundaries, employees can have the freedom to approach their work in their unique ways while maintaining focus on desired outcomes.

Unique Benefits:

Enhanced Creativity: Employees have the space to think outside the box and develop innovative solutions.

Improved Engagement: Freedom empowers employees, making them more invested in their work. Consistency in Results: Accountability ensures that the outcomes align with organizational goals.

Practical Examples:

1. Defining Clear Goals and Boundaries:
   Provide employees with clear objectives while allowing them the flexibility to choose how to achieve them.
   Example: A marketing manager tells their team to increase brand awareness by 20% over the next quarter but allows them to decide the specific strategies (e.g., social media, influencer collaborations, or webinars).
2. Autonomous Problem-Solving:
   Encourage teams to resolve issues independently before escalating them to leadership.
   Example: In a customer support team, employees are empowered to offer discounts or refunds within a set limit without seeking managerial approval.
3. Periodic Check-Ins Without Micromanaging:
   Schedule regular progress updates to ensure alignment without interfering in daily activities.
   Example: A project leader checks in weekly with a development team to review milestones but avoids dictating daily tasks, allowing the team to self-organize.

Outcome:

Employees feel trusted and valued, leading to higher job satisfaction and innovation, while the organization achieves consistent and focused results.

2. How Small Gestures of Trust Can Unlock Potential

Key Insight:

Trust is the cornerstone of autonomy. Even small actions that demonstrate trust can significantly impact employee confidence, morale, and productivity.

Unique Benefits:

Boosted Confidence: Employees feel empowered and motivated to take initiative. Faster Decision-Making: Teams make quicker decisions without waiting for managerial approval. Strengthened Relationships: Trust fosters mutual respect between employees and leaders.

Practical Examples:

1. Delegating Meaningful Tasks:
   Assign tasks that show confidence in an employee's abilities. Example: A leader entrusts a junior team member with presenting a key client proposal, signaling trust in their skills.
2. Allowing Flexible Schedules:
   Give employees the autonomy to manage their working hours as long as deadlines are met.

Example: A company allows its employees to choose when to work as long as they log 40 hours weekly and complete deliverables on time.

3. Eliminating Excessive Approvals:
   Remove unnecessary bureaucratic hurdles that imply a lack of trust.
   Example: A design team is authorized to finalize creative assets without needing multiple layers of approval for routine tasks.

Outcome:

Employees become more proactive and innovative when they feel trusted, leading to improved performance and stronger relationships with leadership.

3. Encouraging Ownership in Everyday Tasks

Key Insight:

Ownership instills a sense of responsibility and pride in one's work. When employees feel they "own" their tasks, they are more likely to go above and beyond to achieve excellence.

Unique Benefits:

Increased Accountability: Employees take responsibility for their outcomes, reducing the need for constant supervision.

Higher Quality of Work: Ownership motivates employees to deliver their best efforts.

Long-Term Commitment: Employees feel valued and are more likely to stay committed to the organization.

Practical Examples:

1. Assigning End-to-End Responsibility:
   Let employees oversee tasks or projects from start to finish, including planning, execution, and reporting.
   Example: A sales associate is given the full responsibility of onboarding a new client, from initial outreach to post-sale support.
2. Providing Decision-Making Authority:
   Allow employees to make decisions related to their tasks without requiring managerial intervention.
   Example: A restaurant manager empowers chefs to design weekly specials, fostering creativity and a sense of ownership.
3. Recognizing Individual Contributions:
   Acknowledge and celebrate employees' efforts in completing tasks successfully.
   Example: After an employee successfully leads a product launch, the manager publicly acknowledges their role during a company meeting.

Outcome:

Employees develop a deeper connection to their work, take accountability for results, and consistently deliver high-quality outcomes.

Integrated Practical Example: Balancing Autonomy and Accountability

Scenario:

A technology startup introduces a new product development initiative, aiming to balance creativity with timely delivery. The leadership team struggles to ensure innovation without losing focus on deadlines.

Steps Taken:

1. Freedom With Clear Objectives:
   The team is given the goal of launching an MVP (Minimum Viable Product) in six months but has full autonomy to decide its features and design.
2. Building Trust Through Delegation:
   Each team member is entrusted with a specific responsibility, such as user interface design or backend functionality, with the authority to make decisions within their domain.
3. Fostering Ownership:
   Team members are responsible for presenting weekly updates, including successes and challenges, and proposing solutions for any delays.
4. Encouraging Recognition:
   Leadership celebrates team milestones, such as completing the first prototype, during company wide meetings.

Outcome:

The team delivers the MVP ahead of schedule, incorporating innovative features that exceed expectations. Employees feel empowered by autonomy and motivated by the recognition of their ownership.

Key Takeaways

1. Freedom and Focus Must Coexist:
   Employees thrive when they have autonomy within the structure of clear objectives and account ability.
2. Trust Unlocks Potential:
   Small gestures of trust empower employees, fostering innovation, confidence, and faster decision making.
3. Ownership Drives Excellence:
   Encouraging ownership in daily tasks motivates employees to deliver high-quality outcomes and take pride in their work.

By striking the right balance between autonomy and accountability, organizations create a culture of trust, innovation, and responsibility. This approach empowers individuals while ensuring alignment with organizational goals, unlocking shared potential and driving long-term success.

7

DIVERSITY OF THOUGHT: STRENGTH IN DIFFERENCES

Diversity of thought is the ability to harness unique perspectives, experiences, and approaches to drive creativity, innovation, and problem-solving. When organizations embrace differences and cultivate a culture of inclusivity, they unlock the full potential of their teams. This section explores why diverse perspectives matter, how to create an inclusive culture, and how individual strengths contribute to collective success.

1. Why Every Perspective Matters

Unique Insight:

Diverse perspectives foster innovative solutions by challenging conventional thinking. Every individual's unique background, experiences, and ideas contribute to a broader understanding of problems and opportunities, leading to better decisions and outcomes.

Key Benefits:

Enhanced Creativity: Diverse viewpoints inspire out-of-the-box thinking.

Better Decision-Making: Teams with varied perspectives consider multiple angles, reducing blind spots.

Increased Employee Engagement: When employees feel their voices are valued, they are more motivated to contribute.

Practical Examples:

1. Multidisciplinary Brainstorming Sessions:
   A company includes employees from different departments in product brainstorming sessions to gain diverse insights.
   Example: An IT team invites marketing and customer service employees to discuss a new app feature. The marketing team offers insights on consumer behavior, while customer service highlights common user pain points.
2. Empowering Diverse Teams:
   Leadership assigns diverse team members to solve complex challenges, leveraging their unique strengths.
   Example: A healthcare organization includes clinicians, administrative staff, and IT experts in a task force to improve patient scheduling, leading to a system that is both efficient and patient friendly.
3. Learning From Differences:
   Leaders actively encourage discussions where employees challenge each other's assumptions.
   Example: A team working on sustainability projects includes members with backgrounds in engineering, social work, and

economics, resulting in a comprehensive strategy addressing environmental, social, and financial factors.

2. Simple Steps to Create a Culture of Inclusivity

Unique Insight:
Inclusivity is not about having diversity on paper; it's about creating an environment where every individual feels valued, respected, and empowered to share their ideas. Inclusivity fosters trust, collaboration, and belonging, which are critical for maximizing the benefits of diversity.

Key Steps:

1. Encourage Open Communication:
   Create safe spaces where employees feel comfortable expressing their ideas without fear of judgment.
   Example: A tech startup holds weekly "idea sharing" meetings where every employee, regardless of seniority, can pitch ideas for improvement.
2. Recognize and Address Bias:
   Provide training to help employees and leaders recognize unconscious biases that might hinder inclusivity.
   Example: A company introduces bias-awareness workshops, helping hiring managers focus on skills and potential rather than stereotypes during recruitment.
3. Celebrate Diversity Through Representation:
   Ensure leadership teams reflect the diversity of the workforce, inspiring inclusivity across all levels.

Example: A manufacturing company creates a leadership mentorship program for underrepresented groups, improving diversity in decision-making roles.

4. Tailor Policies to Diverse Needs:
   Adapt policies to accommodate different cultural, personal, or professional needs.
   Example: A multinational corporation offers flexible holidays, allowing employees to take time off during culturally significant events.
5. Foster Collaborative Opportunities:
   Design projects and activities that encourage cross-functional and cross-cultural collaboration.
   Example: An international company creates virtual "cultural exchange" days where employees from different regions share their traditions, fostering connection and understanding.

3. Turning Individual Strengths Into Team Success

Unique Insight:

Diverse teams succeed when individual strengths are recognized, valued, and leveraged in a collaborative framework. Leaders must identify these strengths and align them with team objectives, ensuring each member contributes meaningfully to collective success.

Key Benefits:

Increased Productivity: When employees use their strengths, they perform at their best. Stronger Collaboration: Teams learn to appreciate and rely on each other's unique abilities. Higher

Innovation Rates: Combining different skill sets and perspectives drives creative solutions.

Practical Examples:

1. Strength-Based Team Assignments:
   Assign roles based on individual expertise and passions to maximize productivity and satisfaction.
   Example: A project team designing a new website assigns a tech-savvy member to handle backend development, a creative member to work on design, and a detail-oriented member to manage quality assurance.
2. Cross-Training and Skill Sharing:
   Encourage employees to learn from each other's strengths, building mutual respect and broadening skill sets.
   Example: In a retail company, customer-facing employees learn basic inventory management from warehouse staff, while warehouse workers learn customer service techniques.
3. Celebrating Individual Contributions:
   Acknowledge and reward the unique contributions of team members to highlight the importance of diverse skills.
   Example: A marketing team launches a successful campaign, and the manager recognizes the data analyst's ability to identify trends, the designer's creativity, and the writer's persuasive messaging in a team meeting.
4. Creating Balanced Teams:
   Build teams that combine analytical thinkers, creative visionaries, and practical executors to ensure well-rounded solutions.

Example: A product development team includes engineers, customer support agents, and business strategists, ensuring technical feasibility, user-centric design, and market relevance.

Integrated Practical Example: Harnessing Diversity of Thought

Scenario:

A financial services firm faces declining client satisfaction due to outdated processes. Leadership realizes that siloed decision-making has led to stagnation and decides to leverage the diversity of thought within the organization.

Steps Taken:

1. Engaging Diverse Perspectives:
   Leadership forms a cross-departmental task force, including IT, sales, customer support, and compliance, to redesign client engagement strategies.
2. Creating a Safe Space for Ideas:
   Team meetings emphasize openness, encouraging each member to share their perspective. Sales staff highlight client frustrations, IT proposes automated solutions, and compliance ensures the strategy aligns with regulations.
3. Leveraging Individual Strengths:
   Each member takes responsibility for a specific aspect of the strategy based on their expertise. For example, IT handles tech implementation, while sales refines communication strategies.
4. Celebrating the Outcome:
   Once the new process improves client satisfaction scores by 30%, leadership publicly acknowledges the contributions of the diverse team, reinforcing the value of collaboration.

Outcome:

The firm creates a client engagement strategy that is both efficient and user-friendly, leveraging the unique strengths of its diverse workforce.

Key Takeaways

1. Every Perspective Adds Value:
   Embracing diverse viewpoints drives innovation, reduces blind spots, and improves decision-making.
2. Inclusivity Creates Belonging:
   Simple steps like open communication, representation, and bias training foster a culture where everyone feels valued and heard.
3. Collaboration Unlocks Collective Potential:
   By aligning individual strengths with team goals, organizations achieve greater productivity, creativity, and success.
   When diversity of thought is nurtured, differences become a source of strength, enabling organizations to thrive in complex, ever-changing environments.

PART 4

TRANSFORMING THE ECOSYSTEM

A thriving ecosystem in any organization is built on trust, motivation, and mutual respect. Recognition and validation are powerful yet often underestimated tools in fostering such an environment. These small but meaningful gestures can drive engagement, improve morale, and build a culture where everyone feels valued. Let's explore how acknowledgment creates lasting motivation, simple ways to express appreciation, and the transformative ripple effects of genuine recognition.

8

RECOGNITION AND VALIDATION: THE SMALL THINGS THAT MATTER

Detailed Perspective:

Recognition and validation are not about extravagant gestures; they're about making individuals feel seen, heard, and valued for their contributions. Acknowledging someone's effort or achievement reinforces positive behaviors, builds self-esteem, and strengthens the emotional bond between employees and the organization.

Analysis:

1. Human Connection:
   Validation satisfies a fundamental psychological need: the need to feel important and appreciated. When employees feel recognized, they perceive their work as meaningful.
2. Retention and Engagement:
   Employees who feel validated are more likely to stay committed to their roles, reducing turnover and boosting engagement.

3. Reinforcement of Values:
   Recognizing behaviors aligned with organizational values strengthens those behaviors and encourages others to follow suit.

Benefits:

Enhanced Morale: Employees feel motivated to continue contributing at high levels.

Stronger Relationships: Recognition fosters trust and goodwill among colleagues and between employees and leaders.

Higher Productivity: A culture of appreciation inspires employees to go above and beyond in their roles.

Practical Example:

A software development company recognizes a team member's late-night effort in fixing a critical bug by sending a personal email from the CEO. The employee feels valued and motivated to main tain their dedication, and the public acknowledgment inspires peers to take ownership during critical situations.

2. How Acknowledgment Creates Lasting Motivation

Detailed Perspective:

Acknowledgment acts as a psychological and emotional fuel. It validates an employee's efforts and reminds them that their work contributes to something bigger. This recognition has a compounding effect, creating a sustained sense of motivation and purpose.

Analysis:

1. Intrinsic Motivation:
   Recognition activates intrinsic motivators, such as pride and self-worth, making employees driven to excel.
2. Behavioral Reinforcement:
   Consistently acknowledging desired behaviors makes those behaviors habitual across the organization.
3. Emotional Bonding:
   Recognition creates a deeper emotional connection between employees and the organization, leading to higher loyalty.

Benefits:

Sustained Performance: Employees consistently deliver high-quality work, knowing their contributions will be recognized.

Team Cohesion: Acknowledgment fosters mutual respect and collaboration within teams.

Resilience: Employees are more likely to stay motivated during challenging times when they feel valued.

Practical Example:

In a healthcare organization, a nurse is publicly acknowledged during a team meeting for her com passionate care of a particularly difficult patient. The recognition reinforces the organization's values and motivates other staff to embody similar behaviors.

3. Simple Ways to Say, "Thank You" Effectively

Detailed Perspective:

Saying "thank you" effectively doesn't require large gestures; it's about personalization, timeli ness, and authenticity. Tailoring recognition to the individual and delivering it sincerely ensures that it resonates deeply.

Analysis:

1. Personalization:
   Generic acknowledgment feels perfunctory, while personalized messages show genuine attention to the individual's efforts.
2. Timeliness:
   Delayed recognition diminishes its impact. Acknowledging achievements promptly ensures max imum emotional resonance.
3. Consistency:
   Recognition should be regular practice, not reserved for big events or milestones.

Benefits:

Employee Satisfaction: Regular, personalized recognition improves job satisfaction. Stronger Culture: Frequent acknowledgment normalizes a culture of gratitude. Higher Morale: Employees feel valued on a day-to-day basis, not just during annual reviews.

Practical Examples:

1. Personalized Notes: A manager writes a handwritten thank-you card to an employee, detailing how their initiative helped the team meet a critical deadline.
2. Public Acknowledgment: During a virtual town hall, the CEO highlights an employee's innovative idea that saved the company time and money.
3. Peer-to-Peer Recognition: An organization introduces a peer recognition platform where employees can thank colleagues for their support or contributions.

4. The Ripple Effect of Genuine Appreciation

Detailed Perspective:

Genuine appreciation doesn't just affect the recipient; it has a cascading effect on the entire workplace. When employees witness acknowledgment, it fosters a positive culture, inspires similar behavior, and strengthens team bonds.

Analysis:

1. Modeling Positive Behavior:
   Employees who see others recognized are encouraged to emulate those behaviors.

2. Cultural Shift:
   A culture of appreciation reduces negativity, strengthens collaboration, and enhances the overall workplace experience.
3. Emotional Contagion:

Appreciation spreads through teams, creating an environment of collective motivation and trust.

Benefits:

Improved Relationships: Genuine appreciation builds stronger bonds across hierarchical levels. Greater Team Synergy: Teams work more cohesively when gratitude is openly expressed.

Increased Well-Being: Employees feel happier and less stressed in environments where appreciation is commonplace.

Practical Examples:

1. Teamwide Celebrations: A project team celebrates a successful product launch with a team lunch, thanking each member for their unique contributions.
2. Cascading Recognition: A manager acknowledges a team member in a meeting, inspiring other leaders to adopt similar practices.
3. Cultural Initiatives: A company introduces an annual "Appreciation Day" where employees and leaders openly recognize peers and team members for their efforts.

Integrated Practical Example: Recognition in Action

Scenario:

A retail company struggling with high turnover realizes that employees feel undervalued. Leadership decides to implement a comprehensive recognition strategy.

Steps Taken:

1. Immediate Acknowledgment: Managers are trained to provide on-the-spot recognition for ex-cellent customer service.
2. Personalized Gratitude: Employees receive handwritten thank-you notes from their managers for hitting sales targets.
3. Celebrating Team Wins: Monthly team meetings celebrate individual and group achievements, with shout-outs for specific contributions.

Outcome:

Turnover decreases by 25%, employee satisfaction scores improve, and customer service ratings increase as employees feel more engaged and appreciated.

Key Takeaways

1. Recognition and Validation Are Essential:
   Even small gestures like a timely thank-you or public acknowledgment can transform workplace morale.
2. Acknowledgment Drives Motivation:
   Employees who feel valued are more committed, engaged, and willing to go above and beyond.
3. Appreciation Creates Ripple Effects:
   Genuine recognition fosters a positive culture, inspiring others to emulate those behaviors and strengthening team dynamics.

By prioritizing recognition and validation, organizations can create an ecosystem where employees feel respected, valued, and inspired to achieve their best. This not only enhances individual performance but also drives collective success, transforming the workplace into a hub of motivation and collaboration.

9

THE FUTURE OF CREATOR-GROWTH CATALYST SYNERGY RELATIONSHIPS

The relationship between employees and managers is evolving rapidly due to technological advancements, changing workforce expectations, and new workplace dynamics. To remain effective, leaders must adapt, foster trust, inclusivity, and collaboration. This section explores what today's workforce expects from leaders, how to adapt to changing work environments, and the im portance of small, consistent efforts to maintain connection.

1. What Today's Workforce Expects from Leaders

Unique Perspective:

Today's employees seek more than traditional management; they expect leaders who act as men tors, advocates, and collaborators. Employees value empathy, flexibility, transparency, and opportunities for growth over rigid hierarchies or micromanagement.

Key Insights:

1. Empathy and Emotional Intelligence:
   Employees want managers who understand and support their personal and professional challenges.
2. Focus on Development:
   Employees expect their managers to invest in their growth through coaching, mentorship, and skill building opportunities.
3. Transparency and Inclusivity:
   Open communication, fairness, and inclusivity are critical to fostering trust and engagement.

Practical Example:

In a tech startup, employees express frustration over unclear career progression paths. The leadership team responds by introducing regular one-on-one meetings to discuss personal goals and ca reer development plans. As a result, employee satisfaction and retention rates improve significantly.

Benefits:

Stronger Trust: Empathy and transparency build deeper trust between employees and managers.

Increased Engagement: Employees who feel supported and valued are more engaged and productive.

Talent Retention: Investing in employees' development fosters loyalty and reduces turnover.

2. Adapting to Changing Work Environments

Unique Perspective:

The rise of hybrid work models, automation, and globalization requires leaders to rethink traditional management practices. Flexibility, adaptability, and digital fluency are essential for navigating these new paradigms.

Key Insights:

1. Embracing Hybrid Work Models:
   Managers must balance the needs of remote and in-office employees by fostering inclusion and collaboration across both environments.
2. Leveraging Technology:
   Digital tools for communication, project management, and employee well-being must be seamlessly integrated into workflows.
3. Fostering Resilience:
   Leaders should prioritize mental health, encourage work-life balance, and create a culture of adaptability to handle uncertainties.

Practical Example:

A multinational corporation introduces a hybrid work policy where employees can choose their work environment. To ensure inclusivity, managers schedule virtual check-ins and team-building activities, using collaborative tools like Slack and Asana to maintain seamless communication. Productivity remains high, and employees report feeling more balanced and connected.

Benefits:

Higher Productivity: Flexible environments accommodate diverse work styles, improving efficiency.

Stronger Team Cohesion: Digital tools and inclusive practices keep teams connected, regardless of location.

Employee Well-Being: Supporting mental health and balance fosters resilience and long-term engagement.

3. Small, Consistent Efforts to Stay Connected

Unique Perspective:

In a world of rapid change, small, consistent actions often make the most significant difference in maintaining strong Creator-Growth Catalyst Synergy relationships. These efforts build trust, demonstrate care, and reinforce a sense of belonging.

Key Insights:

1. Regular Check-Ins:
   Frequent, informal conversations show employees that their managers genuinely care about their progress and well-being.
2. Personalized Recognition:
   Acknowledging individual contributions regularly makes employees feel seen and valued.
3. Two-Way Feedback:
   Providing constructive feedback while seeking input from employees creates a culture of mutual respect and continuous improvement.

Practical Example:

A retail manager starts holding 10-minute daily stand-ups where team members can share their updates and challenges. These quick, consistent meetings foster a sense of teamwork and allow the manager to address concerns proactively.

Benefits:

Stronger Relationships: Regular touchpoints deepen the bond between employees and managers.

Proactive Problem-Solving: Small, consistent actions prevent small issues from escalating into major challenges.

Continuous Engagement: Employees feel consistently supported and connected to their teams.

Integrated Example: A Vision of the Future

Scenario:

A mid-sized consultancy firm aims to enhance Creator-Growth Catalyst Synergy relationships in response to high attrition rates and employee dissatisfaction with remote work policies.

Steps Taken:

1. Meeting Workforce Expectations:
   Managers are trained to conduct meaningful one-on-one sessions focusing on personal development and empathetic leadership.
2. Adapting to Hybrid Models:

The company adopted a hybrid work policy, using tools like Zoom and Trello to ensureeffective collaborationn.

3. Consistent Connection Efforts:
   Weekly check-ins and monthly virtual coffee chats foster a sense of community and connection.

Outcome:

The firm's employee satisfaction scores rise by 30%, attrition decreases, and team productivity improves as employees feel more supported and engaged.

Key Takeaways

1. Meeting Evolving Expectations:
   Today's workforce demands empathetic, transparent, and development-focused leadership.
2. Flexibility in Change:
   Adapting to hybrid models and leveraging digital tools are essential for thriving in changing work environments.
3. Consistency Is Key:
   Small, consistent efforts—like regular check-ins and recognition—build trust, engagement, and resilience.

By addressing these critical elements, managers can transform employee relationships, fostering loyalty, productivity, and a sense of shared purpose in the evolving workplace.

10

A SHARED VISION FOR SUCCESS

A shared vision serves as the cornerstone of any successful organization. It aligns individual am bitions with collective goals, creating a unified culture were purpose and collaboration drive growth. When mutual respect underpins this shared vision, the result is a workplace that thrives on trust, innovation, and continuous improvement. This section explores how to cultivate a shared purpose, the transformative power of mutual respect, and daily practices that keep the vision alive.

1. Creating a Culture of Shared Purpose and Growth

Unique Perspective:

A shared purpose aligns every individual's role with the organization's mission, creating a sense of belonging and direction. It transforms the workplace into a community were individual growth fuels collective success.

Key Insights:

1. Alignment Through Clarity:
   A well-communicated vision helps employees see how their contributions directly impact organi zational goals.
2. Personal and Collective Growth:
   When employees see opportunities for their development within a larger vision, they become more engaged and committed.
3. Purpose as a Motivator:
   A clear sense of purpose inspires employees to go beyond routine tasks, fostering creativity and resilience.

Practical Examples:

1. Crafting a Unified Mission Statement:
   A startup involves employees at all levels in crafting a mission statement, ensuring alignment and ownership.
   Example: A green energy company's mission to "empower communities through sustainable solutions" motivates employees to innovate eco-friendly technologies.
2. Personalizing the Vision:
   Managers connect individual roles to the organizational purpose during team meetings.
   Example: A retail manager explains how a cashier's efficiency contributes to overall customer satisfaction and retention.
3. Offering Pathways for Growth:
   Provide clear career progression opportunities tied to the company's goals.
   Example: A tech firm introduces mentorship programs where junior developers learn from senior engineers, aligning personal growth with organizational innovation.

Benefits:

Increased Engagement: Employees feel their work has meaning, driving higher levels of productivity.

Stronger Retention: Employees who see personal growth opportunities are less likely to leave. Collective Resilience: A shared vision keeps teams motivated during challenges.

2. Why Mutual Respect Is the Ultimate Driver of Success

Unique Perspective:

Mutual respect is the glue that holds a shared vision together. It fosters collaboration, trust, and psychological safety, enabling teams to work cohesively toward common goals. When employees feel respected, they are more likely to respect others, creating a virtuous cycle of engagement and innovation.

Key Insights:

1. Psychological Safety:
   Mutual respect creates an environment where individuals feel safe expressing ideas, ask questions, and take risks.
2. Empowered Collaboration:
   Teams that respect each other's strengths and perspectives work more effectively together.
3. Conflict as Growth:
   In a respectable culture, disagreements are seen as opportunities for innovation rather than barriers to progress.

Practical Examples:

1. Inclusive Decision-Making:
   Leaders actively seek input from all team members before making significant decisions.
   Example: A marketing team brainstorms campaign ideas, ensuring junior members' ideas are considered alongside senior leaders' suggestions.
2. Respectful Communication:
   Encourage constructive feedback delivered in a way that preserves dignity and fosters improvement.
   Example: A manager addresses an employee's missed deadline by discussing challenges and of faring support rather than criticism.
3. Celebrating Diversity:
   Recognize and leverage diverse perspectives and experiences to enrich decision-making.
   Example: A multinational company creates a platform where employees share how their cultural backgrounds contribute to team success.

Benefits:

Stronger Relationships: Mutual respect builds trust and strengthens interpersonal bonds. Higher Innovation Rates: Respectful collaboration encourages the free exchange of ideas. Reduced Turnover: Employees stay longer in environments where they feel valued and respected.

3. Simple Daily Actions That Reinforce the Bigger Picture

Unique Perspective:

While a shared vision is vital, it's the daily actions that keep it alive. Small, consistent efforts to reinforce purpose, respect, and collaboration transform abstract ideas into tangible outcomes.

Key Insights:

1. Repetition Builds Culture:
   Regularly reinforcing the vision and values embeds them into the organizational fabric.
2. Micro-Interactions Matter:
   Small gestures of appreciation or alignment show employees that their daily work contributes to the bigger picture.
3. Accountability Through Consistency:
   Managers who model shared values inspire employees to follow suit, creating a ripple effect.

Practical Examples:

1. Start Meetings With Purpose:
   Begin team meetings by connecting the agenda to the broader organizational goals.
   Example: A sales manager opens a pipeline review by linking revenue targets to the company's mission of enabling affordable healthcare access.
2. Recognize Contributions Daily:
   Acknowledge individual and team efforts in real-time to show how they align with the vision.

Example: A manager thanks a team member in a Slack channel for resolving a customer issue quickly, highlighting its impact on client retention.

3. Share Success Stories:
   Regularly highlight examples of how the shared vision is driving results.
   Example: A nonprofit shares updates during weekly newsletters about how employee efforts are impacting communities.
4. Model Behaviors:
   Leaders consistently demonstrate the values and behaviors they expect from others.
   Example: A CEO who values collaboration attends brainstorming sessions and actively listens to employees' ideas.

Benefits:

Continuous Alignment: Regular reminders keep employees focused on the shared vision. Increased Morale: Small daily acknowledgments boost motivation and team spirit. Sustained Growth: Consistent efforts ensure long-term adherence to organizational values. Integrated Practical Example: Building a Shared Vision

Scenario:

A mid-sized education company struggles with declining employee morale and a disconnect between individual roles and the company's mission to "empower lifelong learners."

Steps Taken:

1. Creating Shared Purpose:
   Leadership conducts workshops to redefine the mission, involving employees in articulating how their roles contribute to it.
2. Fostering Mutual Respect:
   Managers receive training on active listening, inclusive decision-making, and delivering constructive feedback.
3. Daily Reinforcement:
   Leaders begin every team meeting by sharing how current projects align with the mission. Employee contributions are recognized in newsletters and one-on-one check-ins.

Outcome:

Employee engagement improves, collaboration increases, and the company launches innovative learning programs that receive widespread acclaim.

Key Takeaways

1. A Culture of Shared Purpose Inspires Growth:
   Aligning personal and collective goals fosters motivation, engagement, and innovation.
2. Mutual Respect Drives Collaboration:
   Respectful relationships create trust, enhance teamwork, and enable conflict to become a source of growth.
3. Small Actions Have Big Impacts:
   Daily reinforcements of the shared vision sustain alignment, morale, and productivity over the long term.

By focusing on shared purpose, mutual respect, and consistent reinforcement, organizations can create an environment where employees and leaders work together toward a common goal, driving success for individuals and the collective.

PART 5

TOOLS FOR EVERYDAY SYNERGY

Building synergy in the workplace is an ongoing process that relies on consistent actions, open communication, and self-awareness. The right tools can foster trust, collaboration, and mutual respect, creating a harmonious work environment. This section provides novel insights into practical steps for relationship-building, conversation starters for stronger connections, daily communication practices, and reflective exercises for managers and employees.

11

PRACTICAL STEPS FOR BUILDING BETTER RELATIONSHIPS

Novel Insight:

Strong workplace relationships are not built overnight but through intentional and consistent efforts. These relationships thrive on trust, empathy, and shared experiences. Taking small, deliberate actions every day creates a foundation for long-lasting connections.

Key Insights:

1. Lead With Vulnerability:
   Sharing personal stories or challenges can humanize leaders and foster trust among teams.
   62 Redefining Creator-Growth Catalyst Synergy Synergy

   Co-Architects of Growth

Example: A manager shares a past professional failure during a team meeting, showing that mis takes are opportunities for growth.

2. Prioritize Individual Preferences:
   Recognize that every individual has a unique communication style and adapt accordingly.
   Example: One employee prefers written communication, while another thrives on face-to-face dis cussions. Managers tailor their approach to suit each person's preference.
3. Show Up Consistently:
   Regular check-ins, small gestures of support, and follow-through on promises build credibility over time.
   Example: A leader makes it a habit to start their day by walking around the office (or virtual chan nels), greeting team members, and asking how they're doing.

Practical Example:

A project manager introduces a "buddy system" for new hires, pairing them with experienced team members. This fosters connections and accelerates relationship-building, resulting in improved onboarding experiences and faster integration.

Benefits:

Builds trust and credibility.

Encourages open and honest communication.

Strengthens team cohesion and collaboration.

2. Simple Conversation Starters for Stronger Connections

Novel Insight:

The right conversation starters go beyond small talk and encourage meaningful dialogue. These openers help uncover common ground, build trust, and create genuine connections.

Key Insights:

1. Ask Open-Ended Questions:
   Avoid yes/no questions; instead, encourage team members to share thoughts and experiences. Example: "What's one thing you're excited about this week?"
2. Discuss Shared Goals or Experiences:
   Focus on topics that connect individuals to the organization's mission or team goals. Example: "How do you think our recent project aligns with the company's vision?"
3. Incorporate Fun and Curiosity:
   Lighthearted questions can break the ice and foster a relaxed atmosphere.
   Example: "If you could solve any problem in the world with unlimited resources, what would it be?"

Practical Example:

During a team-building lunch, a manager asks everyone to share the most unexpected lesson they've learned in their careers. This sparks laughter, vulnerability, and bonding.

Benefits:

Encourages authentic conversations.

Builds rapport and camaraderie.

Uncovers new ideas and perspectives.

3. Daily Practices to Enhance Communication

Novel Insight:

Effective communication is a daily habit that requires consistency, intention, and adaptability. Leaders and teams can improve their communication by integrating structured yet simple practices into their routines.

Key Insights:

1. Morning Alignment Huddles:
   Start each day with a 10-minute team check-in to set priorities and share updates.
   Example: A remote team uses a morning video call to outline the day's focus and celebrate small wins.
2. End-of-Day Summaries:
   Encourage employees to summarize their daily accomplishments and challenges.
   Example: A marketing team uses a Slack channel to share one thing they achieved that day and any blockers they're facing.
3. Non-Verbal Cues in Communication:
   Pay attention to tone, body language, and facial expressions, especially in virtual settings.

Example: A team leader ensures their tone remains positive and encouraging during a high-pres sure project discussion.

Practical Example:

A software team adopts "demo Fridays," where team members showcase what they've built that week, fostering open communication and collective learning.

Benefits:

Reduces misunderstandings and misalignments.

Builds a culture of transparency.

Encourages consistent feedback loops.

4. Reflective Exercises for Managers and Employees

Novel Insight:

Reflection is a powerful tool for personal and professional growth. By dedicating time to self assessment and team feedback, managers and employees can identify areas for improvement, cel ebrate achievements, and set goals for the future.

Key Insights:

1. Weekly Self-Reflection Prompts:
   Encourage employees to evaluate their performance and emotional well-being. Example Prompts:
   "What's one thing I did this week that I'm proud of?"
   "What challenges did I face, and how did I overcome them?"

2. Team Feedback Circles:
   Create safe spaces where teams can share constructive feedback with each other.
   Example: A monthly "team reflection day" where everyone shares one strength and one area of improvement for the team.
3. Gratitude Journaling:
   Reflecting on positive experiences fosters a growth mindset.
   Example: Employees list three things they're grateful for at work, such as supportive colleagues or exciting projects.

Practical Example:

A manager conducts a quarterly "personal growth check-in" with each team member, discussing what they've learned, their goals, and how they feel about their progress. These insights are then used to tailor development plans.

Benefits:

Promotes self-awareness and accountability.

Builds a culture of continuous improvement.

Strengthens trust and collaboration through shared reflection.

Integrated Practical Example: A Day of Synergy in Action

Scenario:

A consulting firm wants to improve team communication and collaboration after receiving feed back about misaligned priorities.

Steps Taken:

1. Morning Alignment:
   The team begins the day with a huddle to align on goals and priorities.
2. Midday Connection:
   During lunch, the manager initiates a conversation about what excites each team member about their work.
3. Evening Reflection:
   At the end of the day, employees share their biggest accomplishment in a group chat, fostering a sense of achievement and community.
4. Weekly Reflection Exercise:
   Every Friday, the team fills out a reflection survey to identify successes, challenges, and areas for improvement.

Outcome:

The team experiences improved communication, stronger relationships, and higher alignment with the company's goals.

Key Takeaways

1. Practical Steps Build Trust:
   Regular efforts to connect and align strengthen relationships and foster collaboration.
2. Meaningful Conversations Create Bonds:
   Thoughtful conversation starters encourage authenticity and deeper connections.
3. Daily Communication Habits Drive Transparency:
   Consistent practices like huddles and feedback loops ensure alignment and clarity.

4. Reflection Fuels Growth:
   Reflective exercises empower individuals and teams to improve continuously.

By integrating these tools into daily workflows, organizations can cultivate synergy, ensuring that teams remain connected, motivated, and aligned with shared goals.

12

TURNING FEEDBACK INTO FUEL

Feedback, when treated as a dynamic force, transcends criticism and becomes the foundation for innovation, resilience, and collective evolution. It's a tool that sharpens potential, unlocks hidden strengths, and redefines growth as a shared journey.

1. Tools for Delivering and Receiving Feedback Effectively

Novel Perspective:

Feedback isn't a monologue—it's a dialogue of transformation. Effective feedback creates a cir cular flow of wisdom, connecting intent with impact and fostering a culture of mutual elevation.

The Echo Model: Feedback should resonate. Deliver it in a way that allows the recipient to hear its value, absorb its meaning, and reflect its lessons.

Example: Instead of saying, "Your presentation was disorganized," try: "Your content was insight ful—how can we structure it to make your ideas even more impactful?"

67 Redefining Creator-Growth Catalyst Synergy Synergy

Feedback Maps: Visualize feedback to give it clarity. Create actionable pathways rather than point ing out flaws.

Example: Use diagrams or bullet points to highlight strengths, opportunities, and actionable next steps.

Emotionally Intelligent Feedback: Recognize the emotional state of the recipient and frame feed back to inspire rather than deflate.

Example: Acknowledge effort first: "I see the dedication you've put into this project. Let's explore some tweaks that could make it even stronger."

2. Building Habits of Constructive Criticism

Novel Perspective:

Constructive criticism is an art of refinement, not rejection. It chisels away the unnecessary while preserving and enhancing the core value of the work or effort.

Normalize Feedback Loops: Embed feedback into regular workflows, so it becomes a natural, non threatening part of the process.

Example: In team meetings, dedicate time to "two stars and a wish"—two positives and one area for improvement.

The Balance Principle: Feedback should balance encouragement with challenge. Overemphasis on either can create complacency or defensiveness.

Example: "This solution showcases your creativity. What if we explore integrating this approach with a data-driven strategy?"

Practice Feedback Literacy: Teach teams how to give and receive feedback with intention and respect.

Example: Offer workshops on active listening and delivering clear, actionable insights.

3. Frameworks for Mutual Growth

Novel Perspective:

Feedback isn't just an individual tool—it's a collaborative instrument for mutual advancement. Both giver and receiver should emerge enriched, aligned toward shared goals.

The "Upward Spiral" Model: Feedback should spark iterative improvement. Each cycle builds on the previous, creating compounding benefits.

Example: A designer and client agree on a feedback loop where ideas evolve collaboratively, en suring alignment at every step.

Co-Creation Conversations: Frame feedback as a shared journey rather than a one-sided critique.

Example: "How can we work together to elevate this project?" invites mutual investment in the outcome.

The Reflect and Refine Framework: End feedback sessions by asking the recipient to summarize insights and propose next steps, solidifying learning.

Example: After providing feedback, ask, "What do you think we should prioritize next based on this conversation?"

13

THE SMALL WINS PHILOSOPHY

Progress isn't always monumental. It's often forged in small, consistent triumphs that accumulate into transformative achievements. The small wins philosophy reframes success as a journey of incremental, meaningful steps.

1. Celebrating Incremental Progress

Novel Perspective:

Each small win is a microcosm of greater success. By celebrating them, we cultivate a culture of momentum and possibility, where every effort becomes a building block for larger victories.

The Progress Paradox: Recognize that the smallest forward movement often carries the greatest psychological weight.

Example: A manager celebrates a junior team member for improving one key metric in a challeng ing report, framing it as a step toward mastery.

Milestone Mapping: Break large goals into smaller, achievable milestones and celebrate each step.

Example: A sales team working toward a quarterly target acknowledges every 10% milestone with public shout-outs and team lunches.

Micro-Moments of Recognition: Praise progress in real time to reinforce positive behaviors.

Example: During a brainstorming session, a leader acknowledges an insightful contribution on the spot, motivating others to share ideas freely.

2. Recognizing Effort as Much as Results

Novel Perspective:

Effort is the invisible foundation of success. By valuing the journey as much as the destination, we create a culture that champions perseverance and learning.

Process-Oriented Praise: Highlight the strategies and persistence behind achievements, not just the outcomes.

Example: "Your dedication to testing different approaches has been impressive, and it's clear how much you've learned along the way."

Effort-Energy Amplifiers: Tie recognition of effort to motivation for future actions.

Example: "Your commitment to learning this new tool has set the standard for our team's adapta bility."

Resilience Rewards: Celebrate attempts, even when they don't yield immediate success.

Example: After a failed project pitch, a manager praises the team's creativity and encourages them to refine their ideas for future opportunities.

3. How Small Wins Create Lasting Momentum

Novel Perspective:

Small wins create a psychological flywheel—each success propels the next, building a sense of capability and invincibility over time.

Compounding Confidence: Acknowledge small wins to build self-belief that empowers employees to tackle bigger challenges.

Example: After successfully leading a small meeting, an employee is encouraged to take on a larger presentation, progressively building leadership skills.

Momentum-Tracking Rituals: Create rituals to reflect on and track small wins, reinforcing forward movement.

Example: A development team ends every sprint by listing three achievements, no matter how minor, in a "wins board."

Celebrate the Journey, Not Just the Finish Line: Highlight how incremental progress feeds into long-term success.

Example: In a fitness startup, the team celebrates every 100 new subscribers as part of their journey toward their annual growth target.

Integrated Practical Example: Turning Feedback and Small Wins Into Culture Scenario:

A mid-sized consulting firm struggles with employee burnout and disengagement. Leadership de cides to implement feedback and small wins strategies to reinvigorate the team.

Steps Taken:

1. Feedback for Growth:
   Managers introduce monthly "growth dialogues," where feedback is framed as a co-creative con versation focusing on strengths and areas for growth.
2. Celebrating Effort:
   Weekly team huddles include "effort stories," where employees share how they overcame chal lenges, regardless of the outcome.
3. Tracking Wins:
   The firm introduces a "small wins journal" where teams document progress on projects daily.

Outcome:

Employee engagement increases as individuals feel supported and recognized. Small wins and constructive feedback create an environment of continuous improvement and positivity, leading to better project outcomes and a stronger culture.

Key Takeaways

1. Feedback as Fuel for Growth:
   Constructive, emotionally intelligent feedback fosters mutual development and iterative progress.
2. The Power of Incremental Progress:
   Celebrating small wins builds momentum, confidence, and a culture of perseverance.

3. The Ecosystem of Recognition:
   When feedback and small wins are embedded into daily practices, they create a workplace where continuous learning and positivity thrive.

By adopting these novel perspectives, organizations can turn everyday moments into powerful catalysts for collective success, ensuring a culture of growth, innovation, and fulfillment.

PART 6

SUPPLEMENTARY MATERIALS

Case Studies of Simple Actions with Big Impacts

Sometimes, small, deliberate actions can create monumental shifts in relationships, trust, and collaboration. These micro-moments, when executed consistently and thoughtfully, ripple through teams, influencing culture and outcomes. Below are detailed case studies illustrating how seemingly minor actions transformed workplace dynamics and strengthened relationships.

1. A CEO's Habit of Handwritten Notes: Building Trust and Morale

Case Study:

A large financial services firm was facing declining employee morale after a merger. Employees felt disconnected from leadership and uncertain about their future in the new organization.

Action Taken:

The CEO decided to write handwritten thank-you notes to employees who went above and beyond in their roles. These notes highlighted specific contributions, such as helping integrate teams or exceeding client expectations.

Outcome:

Improved Morale: Employees shared the notes with colleagues, creating a sense of pride and recognition throughout the organization.

Rebuilt Trust: Employees began to see leadership as approachable and invested in individual contributions.

Increased Engagement: Recognized employees were motivated to continue their high performance, inspiring peers to strive for similar acknowledgment.

Lesson:

Personalized and specific recognition, even through simple gestures, fosters a deep emotional connection between employees and leadership.

2. The 2-Minute Daily Check-In: Strengthening Team Dynamics

Case Study:

A software development team working on a tight deadline began experiencing friction and mis communication. Tensions escalated, leading to inefficiencies and missed deliverables.

Action Taken:

The team leader introduced a daily 2-minute check-in where every team member shared:

1. What they were working on.
2. What they needed help with.
3. A non-work-related highlight of their day.

Outcome:

Improved Communication: Sharing updates daily reduced miscommunication and clarified prior ities.

Enhanced Team Bonding: Personal highlights fostered a sense of camaraderie and trust among team members.

Increased Efficiency: The team resolved blockers faster and improved collaboration, meeting the project deadline successfully.

Lesson:

Small, consistent actions like brief check-ins can resolve conflicts, build trust, and improve team cohesion in high-pressure environments.

3. Open Door Policy with a Twist: Creating Psychological Safety

Case Study:

A retail company with a high employee turnover rate noticed that junior employees rarely voiced concerns or ideas due to fear of judgment or retribution.

Action Taken:

The HR director implemented an open-door policy but added a unique twist: every Friday, the director sat in the company cafeteria for an hour, inviting employees to join them for casual, anon ymous conversations about challenges and suggestions.

Outcome:

Enhanced Psychological Safety: Employees felt more comfortable sharing concerns without formalities, leading to actionable feedback.

Increased Retention: Employees appreciated the accessible leadership style, reducing turnover.

Improved Processes: Suggestions led to changes like clearer onboarding practices and more flex ible shift scheduling.

Lesson:

Creating informal opportunities for open dialogue fosters psychological safety and trust, empow ering employees to share ideas without fear.

4. The Gratitude Wall: Building a Culture of Appreciation

Case Study:

A mid-sized healthcare organization wanted to boost employee morale in a high-stress environment. Leadership noticed a lack of recognition for small but impactful contributions.

Action Taken:

They introduced a "Gratitude Wall" in the breakroom, where employees could write thank-you notes to colleagues for acts of kindness, teamwork, or exceptional effort.

Outcome:

Strengthened Relationships: Employees felt appreciated by peers and formed deeper connections.

Cultural Shift: The visible expressions of gratitude inspired others to adopt a more positive and supportive mindset.

Reduced Stress: Recognizing small wins and kindness created a more uplifting work environment.

Lesson:

Encouraging peer-to-peer recognition cultivates a culture of appreciation, reducing stress and fos tering camaraderie.

5. Manager's 15-Minute Career Conversations: Driving Engagement

Case Study:

An IT services company experienced disengagement among mid-level employees, many of whom felt their career growth had stagnated. Managers were too focused on operational priorities to ad dress these concerns.

Action Taken:

One manager began scheduling 15-minute bi-weekly "career conversations" with each team mem ber. The discussions focused on:

1. Long-term career goals.
2. Current skills they wanted to develop.
3. Opportunities within or beyond their current role.

Outcome:

Renewed Engagement: Employees felt their growth mattered, leading to higher motivation and productivity.

Reduced Turnover: The manager identified opportunities for internal mobility, retaining top talent.

Improved Team Morale: Employees began viewing the manager as a mentor invested in their success.

Lesson:

Short but focused career conversations demonstrate a manager's investment in employees' futures, boosting engagement and retention.

6. Coffee Roulette: Breaking Down Silos

Case Study:

A multinational firm struggled with siloed departments, limiting cross-functional collaboration and innovation. Employees rarely interacted with colleagues outside their immediate teams.

Action Taken:

The HR department introduced "Coffee Roulette," where employees were randomly paired for 15- minute virtual, or in-person coffee chats every two weeks.

Outcome:

Improved Collaboration: Employees built relationships across departments, leading to cross-functional project ideas.

Fostered Inclusivity: Employees at all levels, including junior staff, interacted with senior leader ship, creating a more inclusive culture.

Sparked Innovation: New ideas emerged from unexpected pairings, such as marketing collaborating with IT to streamline customer feedback analysis.

Lesson:

Facilitating informal cross-department interactions can spark innovation and create a more cohesive organizational culture.

7. The Weekly "Win Session": Cultivating Momentum

Case Study:

A sales team in a competitive industry struggled with burnout due to relentless performance pressure. Motivation waned as team members felt their efforts were undervalued unless they achieved big wins.

Action Taken:

The sales manager implemented a weekly "win session" where the team celebrated small victories, such as reaching out to a challenging prospect or learning a new skill.

Outcome:

Boosted Morale: Recognizing incremental progress reminded employees that every effort mattered.

Increased Productivity: Employees felt motivated to achieve more, knowing even small wins would be celebrated.

Enhanced Team Spirit: The sessions fostered a culture of collective celebration and encouragement.

Lesson:

Recognizing small wins can create lasting momentum, inspiring teams to stay motivated even during challenging periods.

Key Takeaways

1. Micro-Actions Create Macro-Impact: Small gestures like handwritten notes or daily check-ins have a profound ripple effect on morale, trust, and productivity.

2. Consistency Matters: Regularly applying small actions—like gratitude walls or career conversations—builds a sustained culture of positivity and engagement.
3. Inclusion Is Key: Informal initiatives, such as Coffee Roulette or open-door policies, create psychological safety and foster cross-departmental collaboration.

By integrating these simple yet impactful actions, organizations can transform relationships, im prove employee engagement, and build a thriving workplace culture.

GLOSSARY

A paradigm shift where employees and managers collaborate as equal contributors in shaping success, fostering innovation, and driving organizational growth.

ACKNOWLEDGMENTS AND GRATITUDE

As I bring this book to completion, I find myself deeply humbled by the countless individuals whose guidance, inspiration, and support have been instrumental in shaping its pages. Writing this book has been a journey of reflection, learning, and growth, and I owe a great deal of gratitude to the many co-architects of this process.

To my family: Your unwavering belief in me has been the bedrock of my strength. Your love, patience, and encouragement have sustained me through late nights of writing and moments of doubt. Thank you for being my greatest champions and my constant source of inspiration.

To my mentors: Your wisdom and insights have left an indelible mark on my perspective. You have shown me what it means to lead with purpose, humility, and empathy, and for that, I am forever grateful. Thank you for pushing me to think deeper and reach higher.

To my colleagues and collaborators: The workplace is where theory meets practice, and it is in those shared experiences that this book was born. Thank you for challenging my ideas, sharing your perspectives, and reminding me of the profound impact that relationships can have on success.

To the readers: This book is for you. Your curiosity, ambition, and desire to create meaningful connections inspired every word. I hope that the concepts and stories within these pages resonate with you and empower you to transform your relationships into catalysts for growth.

To the unsung heroes: To those who encouraged me with a kind word, provided me with a much needed spark of inspiration, or simply shared a moment of connection—your contributions, how ever small they may seem, have been invaluable. Thank you for being part of this journey.

Finally, to the process itself: Writing this book has been as much a journey of self-discovery as it has been an exploration of ideas. I am grateful for the challenges, the breakthroughs, and the op portunity to grow as both a thinker and a creator.

This book is the result of countless contributions from a network of incredible people, and it stands as a testament to the power of collaboration and connection. Thank you for helping me bring this vision to life. Together, we are all co-architects of growth.

With deepest gratitude,

Biswajit Salui